From the gardening library of
WILLIAM W. LANIGAN

GARDENS FOR SMALL COUNTRY HOUSES

Gertrude Jekyll (1843-1932) studied painting as a young girl and went on to fulfil many commissions, enjoying considerable reputation as an artist and craftswoman before she became a 'gardener'. A friend and collaborator of Edwin Lutyens, she contributed many articles on gardening to *Country Life*. Her published works include *Wood and Garden* (also available in Papermac), *Colour Schemes for the Flower Garden*, *Home and Garden*, *Garden Ornament*, *Roses for English Gardens*, *Lilies for English Gardens*, *Wall, Water and Woodland Gardens* and *A Gardener's Testament*.

Sir Lawrence Weaver (1876-1930) had a distinguished and varied career, but it was as an architect, architectural critic, and more especially as architectural editor of *Country Life* from 1910-1916 that he is best remembered today. A prolific writer, his works include *Small Country Houses of Today*, *Houses and Gardens by E.L. Lutyens* and the *Country Life Book of Cottages*.

GARDENS FOR SMALL COUNTRY HOUSES

BY

GERTRUDE JEKYLL & LAWRENCE WEAVER

ANTIQUE COLLECTORS' CLUB

Published for the Antique Collectors' Club by the Antique Collectors' Club Ltd.

Printed in England by Antique Collectors' Club Ltd., Woodbridge, Suffolk

Gardens for Small Country Houses.

INTRODUCTION TO THE ANTIQUE COLLECTORS' CLUB EDITION

More than any other single volume *GARDENS FOR SMALL COUNTRY HOUSES* contains the substance of a legend: with classical *Country Life* images and calm and decorous prose, the pages reveal that dream time at the very end of the last century and the beginning of this one, when the Arts and Crafts Movement had evolved into country house architecture and then found its most delightful expression in the making of gardens. The original title page of this book indicated a threefold pedigree, the joint authors, Gertrude Jekyll and Lawrence Weaver, and the publishing house, Country Life. All three are significant, as I shall hope to show, but pride of place must go to Miss Jekyll, for it is with her life and art that this book is most closely entwined. When it was first published in 1912 she was sixty-nine years' old, with most of her books on the art and practice of gardening behind her;[1] *GARDENS FOR SMALL COUNTRY HOUSES* enlarges our vision of her world, for here you will find houses by Lethaby, Prior, Detmar Blow, and Baillie Scott as well as Edwin Lutyens, and also other people who were as rich and talented as she was and so able to live according to her high ideals. *GARDENS FOR SMALL COUNTRY HOUSES* is brought into context within the framework of her life, and I hope that it will be all the more appreciated for a brief explanation of how it came to be written.

Gertrude Jekyll was born in London in 1843, into a cultured, upper middle class family; when she was still a small child her parents, Edward and Julia Jekyll, took their family to live at Bramley Park, just south of Guildford in Surrey. Maybe this release of a spirited five-year-old into a large and beautiful garden and park triggered off her passion for her home county, but however it came about, this great bond between Gertrude Jekyll and south-west Surrey was to influence the rest of her life. It is no accident, therefore, that Chapter I of this book is devoted to *Millmead*, in Snowdenham Lane, Bramley, the small house that Lutyens built for her in 1904, both because she wished to prove that good design need not be the prerogative of the large house and garden, but also because she found the land overlooked her old home and the scene of "childish primrose-picking rambles" and she could not resist it. Her treatment of the long, thin plot is refreshing, especially in the light of recent contortions to disguise such plots as anything but long and thin, and her simplest planting is shown most effectively. She never lived in *Millmead* but owned and let it for several years; both house and garden are still in good condition and the forecourt planting of "good green foliage" that she describes is still much as she intended.

After her happy Bramley childhood, she was launched into London society at eighteen to study painting, the first of the artistic pursuits in which she was to become involved with a characteristic thoroughness and hard work. She knew John Ruskin and many of the painters of her day, including G.F. Watts, Frederic Leighton and Burne-Jones: Ruskin's inspiration led her to the belief that painting was not enough, and a meeting with William Morris (then at Red Lion Square) encouraged her to a variety of arts and crafts including embroidery, the working of base and precious metals, especially silver, wood carving and interior decorations, always working to her own designs. Throughout her twenties and

1.   *Wood & Garden*, 1899; *Home & Garden*, 1900; *Lilies for English Gardens*, 1901; *Wall & Water Gardens*, 1901; *Roses for English Gardens*, 1902; *Flower Decoration for the House*, 1907; *Colour in the Flower Garden*, 1908; *Children & Gardens*, 1908.

thirties she led a busy artistic life combined with travelling all over Europe and Britain, with always an interest in other peoples' gardens, especially the Renaissance gardens of Italy, the Moorish gardens of Spain and the good 'old' gardens of England and Scotland — of which Berkeley Castle, Edzell Castle, Pitmedden House and Montacute were her special favourites. Thus the chapters that follow on steps and stairways, balustrades and walls, yew hedges, gates and garden houses, vividly reflect her 17th century tastes and her knowledge of these features, though Lawrence Weaver probably added the constructional details.

By the time she reached her late thirties, Gertrude Jekyll enjoyed a considerable reputation as an artist and craftswoman and she had fulfilled many commissions, especially for embroideries and silverwork; however, at this time it became certain that her weak and short-sighted eyes could not endure the strain of such close, fine work for much longer, and this realisation, together with the death of her father, combined to alter the direction of her life. The Jekylls had left Bramley in 1868 to live in a house that Edward Jekyll inherited at Wargrave in Berkshire, but when he died in 1876 there was no need for exile from Surrey to last any longer, and Gertrude, her mother and her brother Herbert (the only brother still living at home) moved into their new house on Munstead Heath, just south of Godalming, in the late summer of 1878. Now that she was back in her beloved Surrey, London and travelling gradually lost their appeal, and Gertrude Jekyll settled into her 'second' life as a gardener. She made the garden for her mother's house, and then bought the "fifteen acres of the poorest possible soil" across, the road, which masquerades in Chapter V as "A Garden in West Surrey", but is of course her own, magical *Munstead Wood.* I can add little to her description of the making of her garden, except the emphasis that it was the mark of her integrity that she treated each of the parts 'on their individual merits' and so created the delightful whole, working in total sympathy with the most profound of the artist-craftsman's ideals. Her most beautiful creation, the woodland garden, is briefly but helpfully explained, and finds further echoes in the gardens at *Woodgate* and *High Coxlease* in Chapter II.

Her gardening brought her into what she called "that wonderful company of amateurs", including Ellen Willmott, Dean Hole, Canon Ellacombe and G.F. Wilson, who were the leading members of the Royal Horticultural Society, and to meet the one professional, the most outspoken of them all, William Robinson. She shared much of her garden philosophy with Robinson and started to contribute to his magazine *The Garden.* It was into this life of gardening and writing that the 20-year-old Edwin Lutyens entered on a May afternoon in 1889, when he was introduced to her as a likely architect for the house she wanted to build in her garden. He also had learned to love Surrey in his childhood and their shared interest in the old and traditional buildings that they examined together as the preparation for building her home in Munstead Wood, was the basis of the friendship and partnership in garden making that was to last for the rest of her life. During the 1890s they perfected an understanding of the relationship between house and garden, and of both to their site, that was embellished by Lutyens' games with geometrical design. During the years 1900 to 1910 they transferred both the integrity and the geometry to some of the greatest gardens of their partnership — including Marsh Court, Folly Farm and Hestercombe—which were given a whole book to themselves.[2] Many of the superbly crafted

---

2.   *Houses and Gardens by E.L. Lutyens,* Lawrence Weaver, Country Life, 1913, reprinted 1981 by the Antique Collectors' Club.

features designed by Lutyens are illustrated in GARDENS FOR SMALL COUNTRY HOUSES, but one of the outstanding creations of the partnership, *Deanery Garden* at Sonning in Berkshire, is given a place of honour as the subject of Chapter III, for a very special reason.

Because of her work for *The Garden,* Gertrude Jekyll had met a quiet, inarticulate man called Edward Hudson, whose pursuit of excellence matched the fervour of her own, and who was about to fulfil his dream. He had inherited his family printing firm, Hudson & Kearns, and expanded into the publication of a high quality sporting magazine called *Racing Illustrated:* Hudson's dream was to turn this into *Country Life Illustrated,* a 'paper' of the finest quality devoted to the interests of the English country gentleman and using "the finest pictorial printing machinery available". The first issues of *Country Life,* as it soon became, appeared in January 1897 and Miss Jekyll was the magazine's authority on the "order and beauty of the woodland and garden". Miss Jekyll introduced Hudson to Lutyens, who built *Deanery Garden* for him in 1901, the first of a string of commissions which resulted from Hudson's passion for Lutyens' architecture and the bond between Lutyens and *Country Life* which is still unbroken.

Lawrence Weaver first contributed to the magazine on the subject of leadwork, and then became its Architectural Editor; however it was probably in the intricacies of fine craftsmanship that his special interest lay, and his detailed knowledge is all pervasive in this book. And, as Miss Jekyll hardly ever left Munstead Wood after 1910, I have no doubt that Lawrence Weaver did all the 'leg work'—arranging for the photographs that she wanted to be taken and journeying between London and Godalming to consult her over the editing and design of the book.

Hudson quickly expanded the *Country Life* imprint into book publishing, and though Miss Jekyll's first two books, *Wood and Garden*[3] and *Home and Garden*[4] were published by Longmans, Green & Co., all her later books were published by *Country Life.* In 1921, her portrait by William Nicholson occupied the prestigious title page of the magazine dated January 29th, along with an eloquent paragraph acknowledging that gardening "was touched with the glory of creative art" through her practice and teachings. She remained friends with Hudson for the rest of her life, and in 1928, when she was eighty-five, almost blind and only able to work for a few hours a day, she went to endless trouble to design beautiful planting schemes for his garden at Plumpton Place in Sussex: for Christmas 1929 he sent her a photograph of the garden signed "from one who has been honoured by your kindness and friendship for so many years".

Thus the pattern of GARDENS FOR SMALL COUNTRY HOUSES falls into place; but though the influences of Lutyens and *Country Life* are strongly evident in these pages, Miss Jekyll was far too perceptive to disregard other tastes in gardening and the work of other good garden designers. In particular, the chapter on "Water in the Formal Garden" contains sketches for designs that are almost frivolous compared to Lutyens' restraint with this element, but which she and Lawrence Weaver obviously felt that others might like. The illustrations of the work of other contemporary designers, especially Walter Cave, C.E. Mallows, Inigo Triggs and Thomas Mawson, the first to call himself a 'landscape architect', are especially valuable as they are comparatively rare. And, whilst Lutyens' presence enhanced her appreciation of architecture in the grden, without him there was less

3.   Reprinted with colour illustrations by the Antique Collectors' Club, December 1981.
4.   Reprinted with colour illustrations by the Antique Collectors' Club, January 1982.

to detract from the natural luxuriance and richness of her planting, beautifully demonstrated in her scheme of 1909 for *Highmount* in Fort Road, Guildford, in Chapter VI. This was one of her virtuoso dry-wall gardens, and both the science and the art of her methods are adequately illustrated, which is especially fortunate as this garden, along with most of the others she did in a similar manner, has now gone. Equally inspiring, in terms of highly-textured planting, is *Westbrook* at Godalming, the garden of Chapter IV, which she made with her neighbour and fellow Surrey antiquarian, the architect H. Thackeray Turner. This garden survives.

For all these reasons, as well as the revelation of a thousand delightful details in planting relationships or craftsmanship that will come with the closer acquaintance with this book, *GARDENS FOR SMALL COUNTRY HOUSES* is not only the handbook of a legend, but it is also a useful and practical book, invaluable for the restoration and repair of gardens. Finally, it captures the reality of all the historical and artistic ideas of a garden—''After all, what is a garden for?'' Miss Jekyll asked, at the end of an article on garden history in the *Edinburgh Review* of July 1896. And she is the best person to answer the question—''It is for *delight,* for *sweet solace,* for *the purest of all human pleasures; the greatest refreshment of the spirits of men;* it is to promote *jucundite of minde;* it is to call home over-wearied spirits. So say the old writers, and we cannot amend their words, which will stand as long as there are gardens on earth and people to love them.''

Jane Brown   October
Ashtead, Surrey   1981

CONTENTS

CONTENTS—*continued.*

INTRODUCTION.

Relation of Garden to House—Importance of Preserving or Creating Character—
Misuse of Conifers—Beauty of Native Evergreens—Various Sites—Yew and Other
Hedges—Treillage—Quiet Entrances—Planting at House-foot.

IT is upon the right relation of the garden to the house that its value and the
enjoyment that is to be derived from it will largely depend. The connection
must be intimate, and the access not only convenient but inviting.   The house,
in the greater number of cases, will stand upon a slight platform, not only because it
is better that it should be raised above the ground-level, but also because the making
of such a platform is an obvious and convenient way of disposing of the earth or
sand excavated for foundations and cellars.   It is also desirable to have one wide, easy

FIG. I.—CLOSE CONNECTION OF HOUSE AND GARDEN.

terrace on the sunny side. The plan and sketch (Figs. i. and ii.) show a clever treatment by Mr. C. E. Mallows of a rectangular space of about an acre. The house is near the middle—an advantage on a small plot; it is well bounded laterally by a pergola, walled on its outer side to the east, and by an evergreen hedge, thick and high, to the west. A small loggia is notched into the house itself—one is in the house and yet in

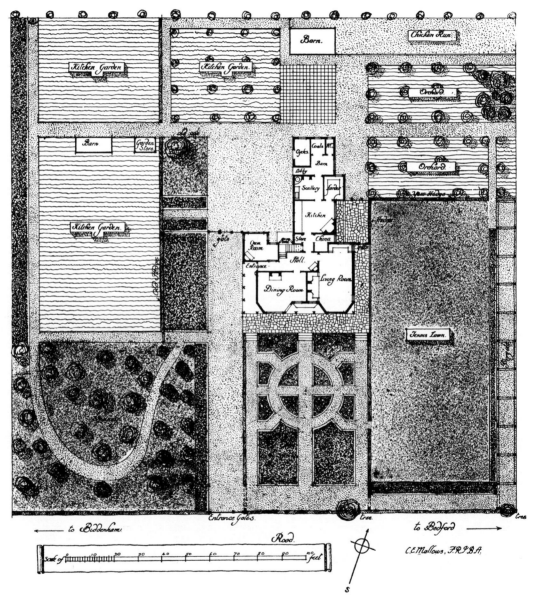

FIG. II.—PLAN OF A GARDEN BY MR. C. E. MALLOWS.

the garden; a step down leads to a comfortable space of terrace; four more steps go directly into the garden. There is a fairly large lawn, a winding walk through a home spinney, and the rest is kitchen garden.

In the arrangement of any site the natural conditions of the place should first be studied. If they are emphatic, or in any way distinct, they should be carefully maintained and fostered. It is grievous to see, in a place that has some well-defined natural character, that character destroyed or stultified, for it is just that quality that is the most precious. Many a hillside site, such as those on wild moorland, has been vulgarised by a conventionally commonplace treatment. Such a place has possibilities that are delightful, and all the easier to accommodate because the poor soil imposes certain conditions and restricts the choice of plants. There are natural gardens in these places, and especially natural groves, that cannot be bettered in the way of consistent and harmonious planting by any choice from a nursery catalogue. Such a region is a hillside clothed with juniper, holly, birch, mountain ash, scrub oak and Scotch fir, in delightfully spontaneous grouping, with undergrowth of bracken and whortleberry, and heaths in the more open places, and other delights of honeysuckle, wild thyme, wood sage and dwarf scabious. It is grievous to see this natural and well-adjusted beauty ruthlessly destroyed, a n d c o m m o n nursery stuff, such as laurels and a heterogeneous collection of exotic conifers, put in its place, whereas it may be so well planted with the native trees that are absolutely s y m p a t h e t i c to its own character, with the addition of the hardier of the cistus, brooms and their kindred species, w i t h r o s e m a r y, lavender, phlomis and many another good plant of Southern Europe. So it is with any other place that has a distinct natural character, whether of granite, limestone or slate-rock. All these have their own flora, indicating to the

FIG. III.—YEWS AT SHEPHERD'S GATE.

careful observer the classes of trees and plants that will best flourish and best adorn.

Happily, our newer gardens are no longer peppered over with specimen conifers. Much as we honour those heads of our great nursery firms and others, whose enterprise and practical encouragement of botanical explorers has so greatly increased the number of coniferous trees that we may now choose from, the earlier mistakes in planting have in many cases been disastrous to gardens. About fifty years ago, when they were being raised and distributed, and horticultural taste was at a low ebb, a kind of fashion arose for planting conifers. It mattered not that they took no place in garden design, and that those who planted had no idea what they would be like when full grown; the object was merely to have one each

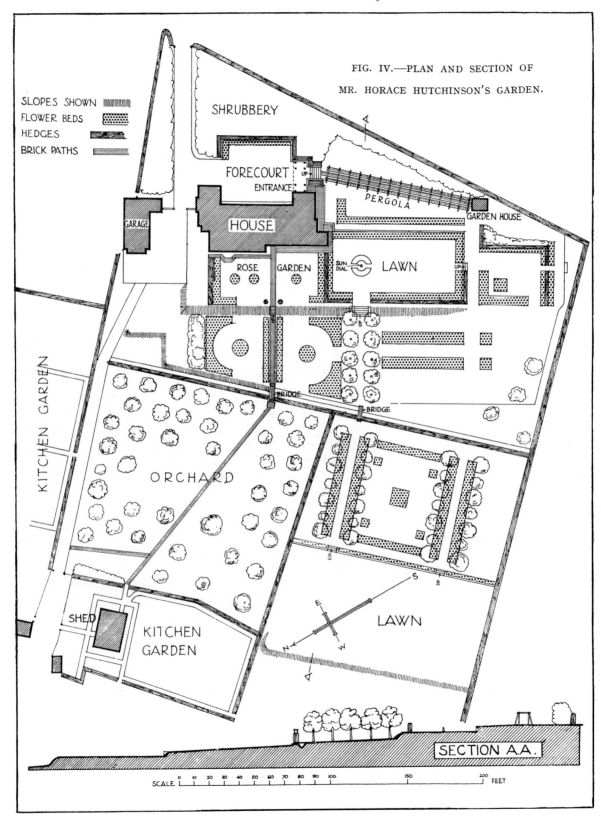

SLOPES SHOWN
FLOWER BEDS
HEDGES
BRICK PATHS

FIG. IV.—PLAN AND SECTION OF
MR. HORACE HUTCHINSON'S GARDEN.

SHRUBBERY

FORECOURT
ENTRANCE
UP

PERGOLA

GARAGE

HOUSE

GARDEN HOUSE

ROSE GARDEN
SUN DIAL
LAWN
UP

BRIDGE
BRIDGE

KITCHEN GARDEN

ORCHARD

LAWN

SHED

KITCHEN GARDEN

N E S W

SECTION A.A.

SCALE 0 10 20 30 40 50 60 70 80 90 100 150 200 FEET

of as many kinds as possible. If the intention had been simply to make a collection from the botanical point of view there would be nothing to criticise; but they were crowded into nearly every garden as exponents of the horticultural taste of the day. Now, when they are approaching maturity of growth, they have either been cut away wholesale, or their owners, of the later generation that has learnt better gardening, look ruefully at the large trees so unwisely planted. In fact, unless space is so great that experimental planting may be done on a large scale, or the foreign trees are so well known in all stages of growth that they can be used with a sure hand, it is safer to trust to our native evergreens and the few European kinds that we have long known. In their way nothing is better than our native juniper, Scotch fir and yew for our sandy uplands; yew also, for chalky soils, and spruce and silver fir for cool hollows. Our noble English yew is nearly always beneficial in the garden landscape. Whether as a trimmed hedge or as a free-growing tree, its

FIG. V.—WALLED GARDEN AT THE MURREL, ABERDOUR, FIFE.

splendid richness of deepest green, and, indeed, its whole aspect, is of the utmost value. No tree is more satisfactory for emphasising important points. Fig. iii. shows two vigorous yews of upright habit in Mr. Horace Hutchinson's garden at Shepherd's Gate, in the old forest region of Sussex. They stand just within the rose garden, above and flanking a flight of steps that leads to lower ground. Standing in the rose garden, and looking between the yews to the half-distant view of wooded hill and down, so typical of the beautiful Ashdown Forest district, they form the frame of the picture, and the tender colouring of the distance is much more fully appreciated than it would be if they were not present. It is a good lesson, and suggestive of what might with great advantage be oftener done in gardens, namely, to frame a distant view in near greenery, either by an occasional arch or by a whole arcade. Roses are well used at Shepherd's Gate; they rejoice in the rich loam of the district, not only growing strongly but also flowering profusely. The whole country is richly wooded, and gives a feeling of protective shelter that is all the

Gardens for Small Country Houses.

more favourable to the well-being of the roses and of the many other good garden plants that flourish in this pleasant place.

Very different as a site is that of The Murrel in Fife, the work of Mr. F. W. Deas, in a country of wide spaces and low, wind-swept hills (Fig. v.). The house and all the outbuildings are closely grouped together, and one feels, with this accomplished architect, how much the whole needed the protection of the great stone wall, whose height, varying from twelve to eighteen feet, rises to one level

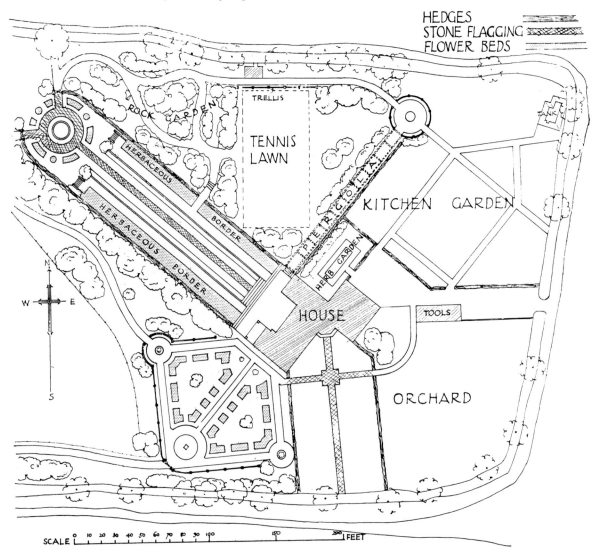

FIG. VI.—PLAN OF GARDEN AT THURSLEY DESIGNED BY MR. E. WHITE.

as the ground falls. It is heavily buttressed, and, like the house, roofed with pantiles.

A site of about two acres at Thursley in Surrey has been cleverly treated by Mr. Edward White (Fig. vi.). House and pleasure garden occupy about half the ground. The entrance path is square with the road, and the house door cuts across an angle formed by the meeting of the main block and the office wing. The

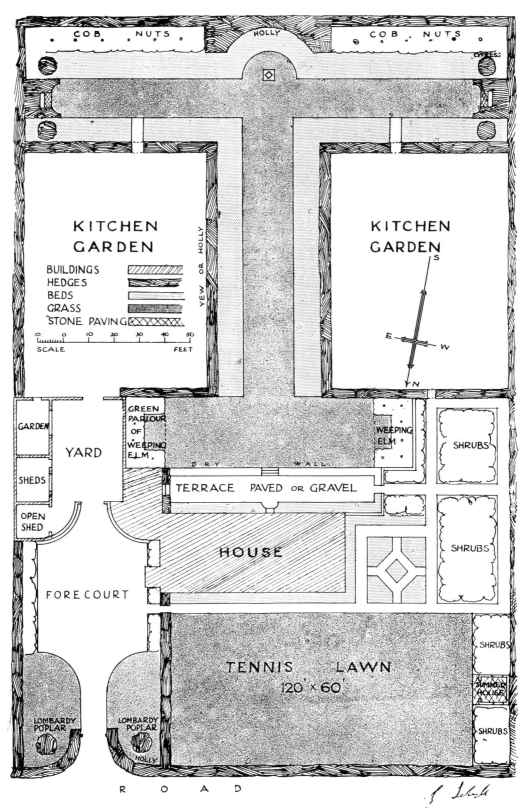

FIG. VII.—A GARDEN OF HARDY FLOWERS ON AN ACRE AND A-HALF.

house, standing diagonally to the road, allows of a longer extension of the flower-borders and the circular garden at the end than could otherwise have been put upon the site. Kitchen garden and orchard are conveniently placed, and the remaining space becomes a useful paddock.

When the site is a bare field, or any place without individuality, the designer has a free hand, but will be wise in choosing something that will be definite, so as to give that precious quality of character. It can only be created by simplicity of aim ; by doing one thing at a time as well and distinctly as possible, and so avoiding complexity and confusion. For instance, if it is desired to treat the ground of a small site of about an acre and a-half as a garden of hardy flowers it may be conveniently laid out as in Fig. vii. The lawn next the terrace has a shady retreat at each end and the wide turf path leading to the further cross path gives the impression of the whole space being given to pleasure garden, while there are still two good plots for

FIG. VIII.—THE DORMY HOUSE, WALTON HEATH : APPROACH FROM GOLF CLUB.

kitchen garden, completely screened, on each side, and space for a play lawn between the house and the road. Tennis players prefer a ground whose longer axis runs north and south, but in this case the exigencies of the site oblige the lawn to run east and west. Such a garden can be worked by a single-handed gardener, with possibly occasional help at pressing times. The green parlours on the front lawn are made with weeping elm, a tree not so much used as it deserves. A slight framework of something like split chestnut is wanted at first to guide the branches laterally to form the roof. As they grow, and then hang down the sides, a complete shelter is formed in a few years.

Yew and holly hedges, such as are shown in this garden, are necessarily costly. The best size to plant, in the case of yew, is from two and a-half feet to three feet, at a cost of five pounds a hundred, putting them eighteen inches apart. Holly of the same height would cost a little more, but the price would be about the same for bushy plants a little under two feet high—a good size to begin with. To make a thick hedge, well furnished to the bottom, yew should have its yearly growth tipped at the ends by at least one-third of the length. Hollies will not want any trimming for the first few years. Such hedges, in favourable conditions, would take from twelve to fourteen years to come to a full growth of six feet to seven feet. Box and

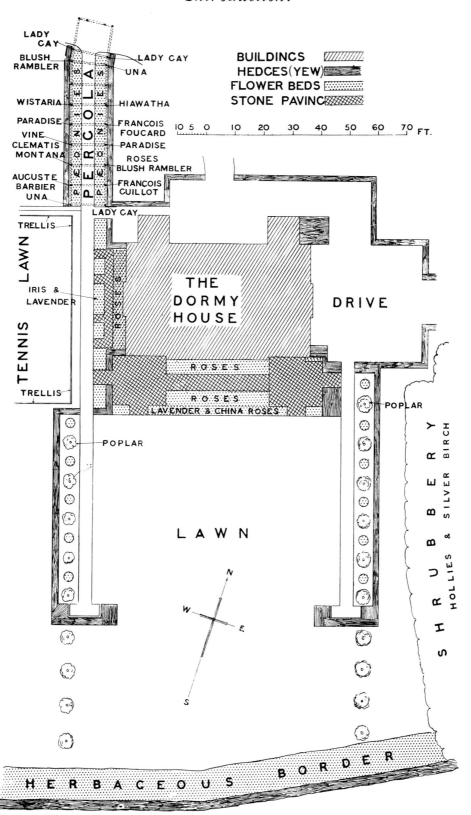

LADY CAY
LADY CAY
BLUSH RAMBLER
UNA
WISTARIA
HIAWATHA
PARADISE
FRANCOIS FOUCARD
VINE
PARADISE
CLEMATIS MONTANA
ROSES BLUSH RAMBLER
AUCUSTE BARBIER
FRANCOIS CUILLOT
UNA

PERGOLA
PERGOLA

BUILDINGS
HEDGES (YEW)
FLOWER BEDS
STONE PAVING

10 5 0   10   20   30   40   50   60   70 FT.

LADY CAY

TRELLIS

TENNIS LAWN

IRIS & LAVENDER

ROSES

THE DORMY HOUSE

DRIVE

TRELLIS

ROSES

ROSES

LAVENDER & CHINA ROSES

POPLAR

POPLAR

SHRUBBERY

HOLLIES & SILVER BIRCH

POPLAR

LAWN

N
W   E
S

HERBACEOUS BORDER

FIG. IX.—DORMY HOUSE : PLAN OF GARDEN.

holly would be rather slower than yew; privet, thorn and hornbeam faster, but as these would have to be cut down nearly to the ground after their first twelvemonth's growth, they would make very little show for the first two years. These are fairly average indications of growth, but on some sites the rate of increase would be considerably more. In the case of the very successful garden of the Dormy House at Walton Heath Golf Club the yews and hollies lately planted have made surprising growth. In this garden the object was to obtain the greatest effect that could be secured while involving the least labour. This has been effected by having several well-arranged flower-borders, and by the use of a quantity of rambling roses on posts and chains. One large double flower-border gives a charming look-out from the club sitting-rooms; another border is at the entrance to the Dormy House (Fig. viii.), whose walls already have a luxuriant growth of vines, the most beautiful of wall ornaments. On its southern side there is a fine piece of stone paving, widening at the two ends into large square platforms (Fig. xi.). The joints are planted with Alpines—perhaps just a little too freely. Many small plants take so kindly to this treatment that the temptation to plant them may easily result in too much invasion of the walking space. A warning as to this over-planting will be found at page 128. A plan showing a suitable amount of planting is given on page 175 (Fig. 247).

FIG. X.—AT THE DORMY HOUSE, WALTON HEATH: THE PERGOLA.

The excellent growth of the yew and holly hedges in the Dormy House garden will, in a few years, give such good protection and sense of enclosing comfort that the absence of built walls will not be felt; but where the cost is not prohibitive, walls of brick or stone are the best of garden boundaries. An ancient wall is in itself a thing of beauty. In the course of long years Nature paints the stone or brick with a number of tender tints, mellowing the whole surface colour; even the passing of twenty years will often show the beginning of this precious *patina*. Then the walls enable us to enjoy many beautiful things, such as myrtle and pomegranate, that are not generally hardy in our climate. Fig. xii. reminds us of the advantage of a wall backing a flower-border. In this case the border might, with advantage, have been wider ; it was, no doubt, made narrow in order that the path should go straight to the doorway at the end. It is one of the many cases in garden arrangement where the course that is easiest is chosen rather than one that is more thoughtful and less obvious. Where neither wall nor hedge is suitable there is the device of treillage, which takes the least room in point of width of any kind of planted fence. This may be either of the carefully designed and constructed kind

as at Ravensbury (Fig. xiv.), where it fitly accompanies a house of eighteenth century character, or it may be of simple oak posts and laths, as at Orchards (Fig. xvi.). Here it is in the walled kitchen garden. Espalier fruit trees are trained against it, and it forms the back on each side of a double flower-border that runs right through the middle of the garden. The posts, standing five feet out of the ground, are set seven and a-half feet apart, and are connected by a top rail, two by one and a-quarter inches, mortised into the posts. The end posts are four inches square ; the intermediate ones three inches. The laths, one and a-half inches wide by half an inch thick, are set square at a distance apart of eleven inches from centre to centre.

Where a rock garden forms part of a scheme it is best placed quite away from the house ; but in many a small garden the only suitable place may be not far from it. When this is the case it can be effectively secluded

FIG. XI.—THE DORMY HOUSE, WALTON HEATH : A PLANTED
PAVEMENT.

by banks planted with shrubs, as shown by the plan in Fig. xiii. The owner of a small place often has the desire of making a good show of flowers —as an amiable form of cheerful welcome—immediately within the entrance. It is a kind thought, but not the most effective way of arranging the garden. It may be taken as a safe rule that the entrance should be kept quiet and, above all, unostentatious. A certain modest reserve is the best preparation for some good gardening on the sunny side of the house, for in most cases the way in will be on the north or east. Labour and horticultural effort are often wasted on flower-borders or summer bedding all along a short carriage-way, which would be much

Gardens for Small Country Houses.

FIG. XII.—FLOWER-BORDER AGAINST WALL.

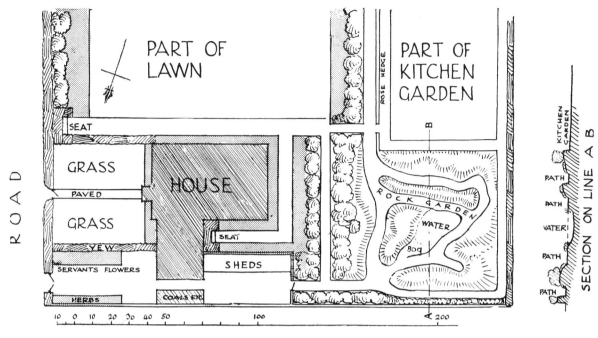

FIG. XIII.—ROCK GARDEN NEAR, BUT SCREENED FROM, HOUSE.

better with a wide grass verge and shrubs alone. It is all the better if the carriage road, often a useless and unpleasantly pretentious feature in a very small place, can be abolished altogether in favour of a flagged pathway. A beautiful treatment of

this kind is shown by Fig. xv., the entrance to Mr. Leonard Borwick's charming home in Sussex, where a flagged path passes through the quiet, unbroken green of well-kept grass.

Another frequent example of waste of effort is where a narrow border at the foot of a house is filled with small plants— annuals or other summer flowers. The border

FIG. XIV.—TREILLAGE AT RAVENSBURY MANOR.

FIG. XV.—BROAD EFFECT OF SIMPLE FLAGGED PATH ACROSS LAWN.

itself is often poorly devised, fussing and dodging in and out among bays and slight projections. It is much better to carry the border straight across, and to fill the spaces next the house with something of solid and shrubby character, such as laurustinus, choisya and escallonia, with a planting, in the narrower spaces and towards the path, of smaller shrubs, such as lavender, rosemary, phlomis, the dwarf rhododendrons, olearias and hardy fuchsias ; then, if front spaces still need filling there is nothing better than the large-leaved megaseas and the stately acanthus in combination with the dark-leaved shrubs, and of southernwood and santolina with the grey.

The title of this volume, " Gardens for Small Country Houses," needs, perhaps, some explanation, because a few of the pictures reproduced belong obviously to large

FIG. XVI.—TRELLIS AT ORCHARDS.

gardens. Although some of the gardens described in the earlier " monograph " chapters (I. to VI.) are of fairly large extent, they mark the increasing tendency to be generous in the provision of garden space round country houses which may fairly be called small. We have not attempted to deal with the little plots which belong to little cottages, as they give scarcely any scope for invention or conscious design. Several scores of photographs have been taken specially for the purposes of the book, but it has not been found possible to rely solely on existing small gardens, known to us, for pictures that would elucidate the points we wished to make. It is fair to claim, however, that no feature has been illustrated which would not be fitting in a small garden when reduced in scale, or which it would be wrong so to reduce. In order

that the range of illustration should be as wide as possible, we have been glad to avail ourselves of several sketches for pools, walls and the like, which Mr. Inigo Triggs has kindly placed at our disposal. To Mr. J. Maxwell Scott and Mr. Charles Yates, among others whose names are given in the text, are due our thanks for the care with which they have made drawings of gardens and their features. The pleasant but not inconsiderable labours of visiting dozens of attractive gardens have been more than repaid by the courtesy and kindness shown by their makers and owners. We may hope that they will have a second harvest in an increased care to secure a right quality in garden design. It is impossible to compress within the limits of such a book more than a fraction of what may be told by pen and picture, but the endeavour has been made to ignore nothing that is essential. G. J.
L. W.

CHAPTER I.—MILLMEAD, BRAMLEY, SURREY.

Site of Ancient Buildings—Shapeless Ground—Terraced in Successive Levels—Steps and Dry-walling—Summer-houses.

SOME old timbered cottages, dating from Jacobean times, standing on a piece of ground in a lane leading westward out of Bramley, were condemned and demolished at the end of the nineteenth century. The ground remained unused for some years, and the part next to the lane, overgrown with docks and nettles, had become a place where neighbouring cottagers found it convenient to throw their household *débris*. In 1904 an old former inhabitant went over it, and found that from halfway down it looked over the wooded grounds of the old home and the half-distant hilly woodland that had been the scene of childish primrose-picking rambles, while the foot of the plot adjoined the green-mill-meadow, in view of some fine, near trees and the rushing millstream, and was within the soothing sound of the working water-mill. It was soon resolved that the land should be bought, and a house built upon it that should not only be worthy of the pretty site but that should also be the best small house in the whole neighbourhood, both for architectural merit and for

FIG. I.—THE FIRST SUMMER-HOUSE. POINT OF VIEW "A" ON GENERAL PLAN (FIG. 4) AND PLANTING PLAN (FIG. 5).

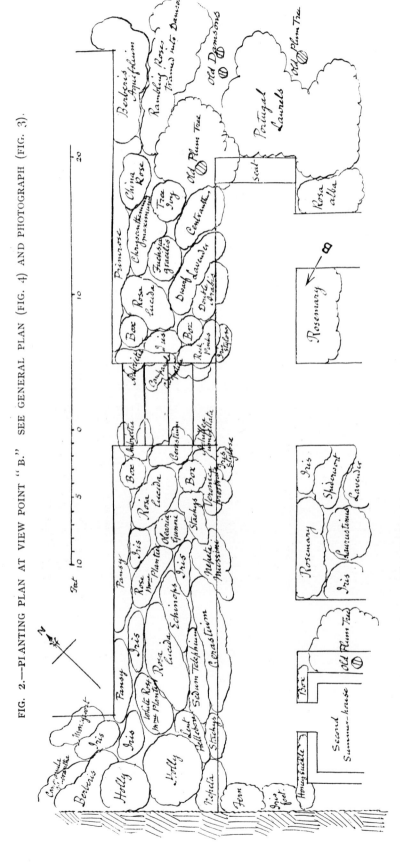

FIG. 2.—PLANTING PLAN AT VIEW POINT "B." SEE GENERAL PLAN (FIG. 4) AND PHOTOGRAPH (FIG. 3).

convenience and comfort. The ground is a little more than half an acre, seventy-seven feet wide and something over four hundred feet deep, on a rather steep slope facing south-south-east. Except for the first hundred feet, which was fairly level, it laid with an awkward diagonal tilt, but it was evident that this could easily be rectified by terracing in a series of levels. The area was not enough to allow of any space for kitchen garden; the whole is therefore given to flowers and shrubs, with one or two small grass plots.

The house, designed by Mr. Lutyens, is reminiscent of some of the small houses of good type built in England under Dutch influence in the early years of the eighteenth century. It is approached from the road by a door in a wall leading into a forecourt. A paved path of Portland stone leads through turf to a wide, flagged platform of the same and to the stone-wrought doorway. The planting of the forecourt is kept rather quiet, with plenty of good green foliage. On the left the wall of the office wing is nearly clothed by a vine, and on the right a rather high wall is covered with the wilder kinds of clematis, montana and vitalba, with a r b u t u s, laurustinus and spiræa lindleyana treated as wall plants, and the borders at the foot have acanthus, m e g a s e a, Lent hellebore, Solomon's Seal and hardy ferns. The flowers are of the modest type, such as columbines and campanulas, the whole intention being to be green and quiet in anticipation of a riot of bright blossom in the main garden on the sunny side of the house. A narrow way, only five feet wide, leads between the house and the western wall to the southern garden. It has been made interesting by the use of some old turned wooden columns that originally formed part of the decorative structure of the wooden ships of the late eighteenth and early nineteenth centuries. Heavy oak beams connect them in pairs across the path, which is paved, partly with the local Bargate stone and partly with a "pitching" of the black ironstones found in the district. A vine planted at the end will in time roof the whole. The garden front of the house, facing south a little east, has a wistaria growing strongly, with good prospect of covering as much of the front as can be allowed,

FIG. 3.—PLANTING OF RETAINING WALL AND BORDER.—POINT OF VIEW " B " ON GENERAL PLAN (FIG. 4) AND PLANTING PLAN (FIG. 2).

while for the further furnishing of the narrow border at the house foot there are escallonia, choisya, rosemary, lavender and iris stylosa.

The garden ground, being in the form of a long strip, the task of the designer was the judicious management of each succeeding level, so that each should have some individuality and distinctive interest, and yet that there should be a comfortable sense of general cohesion. From the wide path in front of the house the ground begins to fall—only a little at first; three steps down are enough. A dwarf dry wall of Bargate stone retains the upper path with its border next the house, and another at the top of the wall; the latter is planted as a rosemary hedge, sweet to the touch

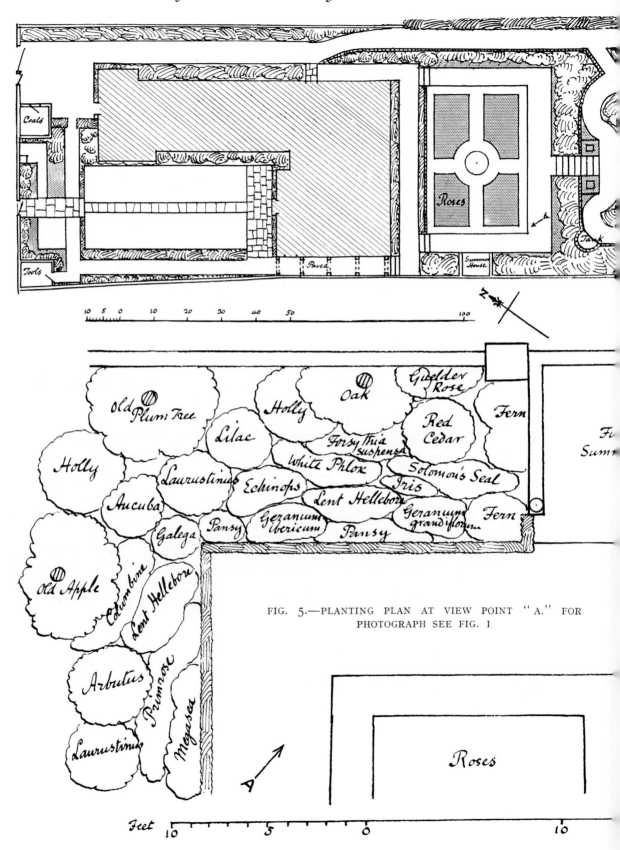

FIG. 5.—PLANTING PLAN AT VIEW POINT "A." FOR
PHOTOGRAPH SEE FIG. I.

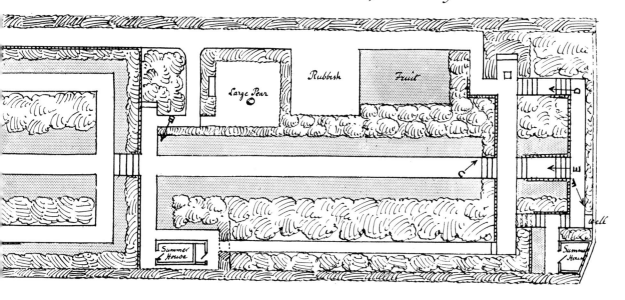

FIG. 4.—MILLMEAD : GENERAL PLAN.

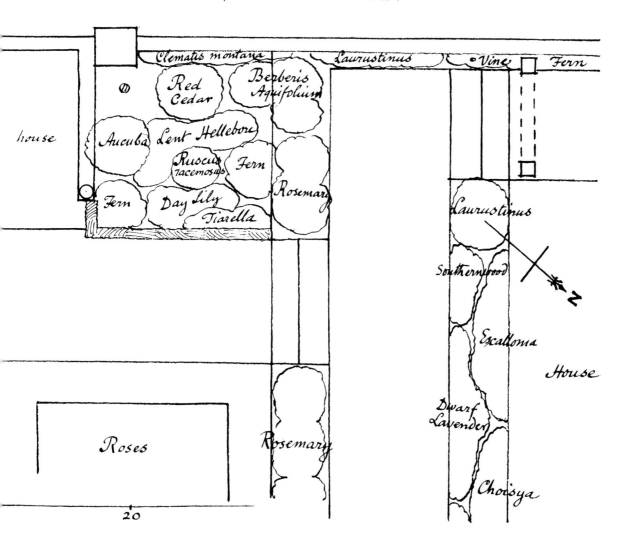

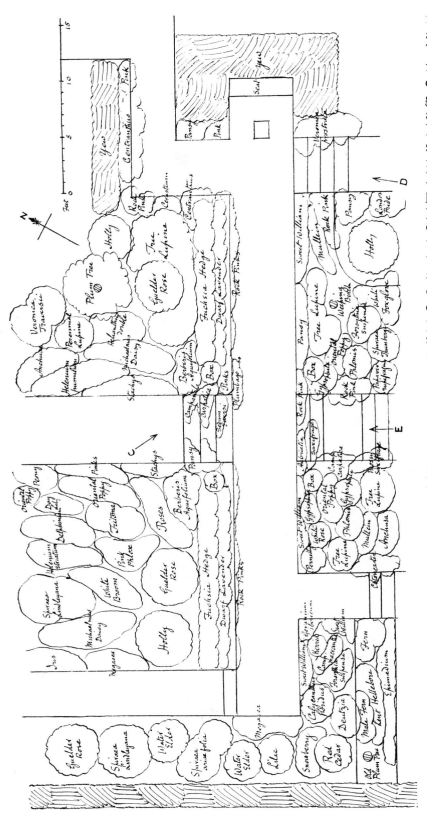

from the path above and the grass below. The lower space is roughly a square, laid out as a little rose garden, with grass paths and a central sundial. Here also is the first summer-house, illustrated in Fig. 1, the arrow and letter A on the general plan (Fig. 4) showing the point of view. It centres the sundial and the grass paths between the rose-beds, and has a pretty view of the church and distant hills, cut as an oval upright picture through the shrubs and further hedge. Outside the grass plot a path runs round three sides, with further borders of shrubs and flowers. A plan is given of the planting of the one on the shady side that contains the summer-house (Fig. 5).

To the next division there is a drop of some feet—a flight of steps leading down to another level, also roughly square, with a central path dividing two large clumps of flower and shrub. The chinks of the steps and the returns of the dry-walling at their sides are bright with aubrietia in May, and the walls to right and left are planted with stonecrops, snapdragons, catmint (*Nepeta*) and other pretty things. At the foot of the steps, squares with flat stone

FIG. 6.—PLANTING PLAN AT VIEW POINTS "C" (SEE FIG. 7), "D" (SEE FIG. 9), AND "E" (SEE FIG. 8).

FIG. 7.—BORDER BY LOWER STEPS. POINT OF VIEW "C" ON GENERAL PLAN (FIG. 4) AND PLANTING PLAN (FIG. 6).

FIG. 8.—THE HOUSE FROM BOTTOM OF GARDEN. POINT OF VIEW "E" ON GENERAL PLAN (FIG. 4) AND PLANTING PLAN (FIG. 6).

edgings hold a pair of hydrangeas. At the western angle a half-round dipping tank is notched into the dry-walling; it is fed by an underground pipe from the pump in the forecourt against the wall to the road, where there is a well that formerly supplied the old cottages. Another retaining wall and flight of steps again lead downwards to a longer piece, the lower part sloping downhill, but levelled right and left. The level of the upper portion was fixed by the presence of a very fine old pear tree. It was given its own little grass plot, and a seat and laurel hedge to surround it on all sides but that of the flower-beds, where the hedge is of lavender. On the western side of the upper part is a little building grouping with, and shaded by, an old plum tree. It was originally intended for a tool-shed,

FIG. 9.—STEPS AND SUNDIAL. POINT OF VIEW "D" ON GENERAL PLAN (FIG. 4) AND PLANTING PLAN (FIG. 6).

but the tenant converted it into a charming little summer sitting-room, and it is now the second summer-house. It is built of oak timber and brick, with a tiled roof, and has the appearance of a miniature old Surrey cottage. On each side of the middle path is the main flower border, forming a continuation of the borders on the level next above. The planting of the retaining wall and border above is shown in the picture (Fig. 3) and plan (Fig. 2), the point of view being from the arrow and letter B on the general plan (Fig. 4). A small path, parallel to the middle one, passes down from the second summer-house between flowering shrubs. At the end of the flower border is another descent of four steps, with a low retaining wall and cross path. The wall is nearly filled with rock pinks ; just at the top is an irregular row of dwarf lavender, the short-stemmed, dark-flowered kind that blooms in July—nearly a month sooner than the larger ordinary lavender—and at the back of this is a hedge of hardy fuchsia. Further flights of steps, on the same middle line, lead down to the lowest level, which is some five feet above that of the meadow. In the narrow border next the meadow are only low shrubs, the better to see the pleasant prospect of mead and millstream, though there are one or two posts for roses and a wild clematis that forms garlands from post to post.

At the southern corner, where there is an odd angle, the third summer-house was built, a wooden structure on a brick foundation, weather-boarded outside and also elm-boarded within. A wide window with casements and lead lights looks out on to the meadow. The little place is of a queer shape, and yet seems roomy. It is thickly roofed with straw thatch. In winter it is curiously comfort-able—always feeling dry and warm. Near it outside is the dipping well, which was built to take advantage of a natural spring, one of the many that feed the stream. It is built up with a Bargate wall about three feet out of the ground. On this a pair of the old ship pillars support a beam with a pulley for the rope that dips and pulls up the bucket. A little tiled roof is built over, now nearly hidden by the growth of a climbing rose

FIG. 10.—THE DIPPING WELL. POINT OF VIEW " F " ON GENERAL PLAN (FIG. 4).

and the wild clematis. Next to the bank and holly hedge which form the eastern boundary, a sloping path on a lower level runs the whole way down, forming a convenient barrow-way with access to each level.

CHAPTER II.—TWO GARDENS IN FOREST CLEARINGS.

*Woodgate, Four Oaks—Virgin Woodland—Emerson and Reginald Blomfield on Design
—High Coxlease, Lyndhurst—Rock and Water.*

THE building of houses and making of gardens on woodland sites raises problems
of treatment and design that need careful thought. Where shall the axe
play and when shall the wielding of it be stayed? Once the trees are down
the outlines of the scheme cannot be altered. As example is more valuable than
precept, we may in this chapter examine two fine gardens that have been stolen from
the wild—Woodgate, Four Oaks, and High Coxlease, Lyndhurst. To few people is
it given to build their homes in such an ideal setting as six acres of virgin woodland,
as it was to Mr. W. H. Bidlake at Four Oaks. Woodgate stands in a triangle between
two roads and once formed part of the great park which the statesmanlike Bishop
Vesey caused Henry VIII. to grant to the Warden and Society of Sutton Coldfield.

About eighty
years ago Sir E.
Hartopp ex-
changed some
land near the
park gates for
that part of the
Corporation's
forest land
which was
known as Lady-
wood, and the
latter is now
being built over,
but the ameni-
ties are well pre-
served. It thus
came about
that Mr. Bidlake
found himself
the owner of a
site that had
never known
the hand of
man, a happy
circumstance
which, joined

FIG. 11.—WOODGATE: STEPS AND GARDEN-HOUSE.

with his skill both in planting and design, has brought into existence a
veritable little garden paradise. The woodland had the unusual charm that
most of its growth was indigenous—oak and holly and silver birch. These
are varied by mountain ash, firs and Spanish chestnut. Beneath the trees
the ground is carpeted in the spring with hyacinths, which are followed by
bracken. When Mr. Bidlake went to Woodgate the soil had never been

disturbed. It consisted of red sand and gravel with scarcely any admixture either of clay or lime, and over it, separated by a sharp line of demarcation, was a top layer of black vegetable leaf-mould six inches thick, the spoil of unnumbered autumns. In the mixture of this mould with the sand rhododendrons grow with extreme freedom owing to the absence of lime, as a noble bank of flowers at the north-east corner of the garden testifies. For many garden denizens this mixture proved too vigorously acid, and for about two years it killed almost everything that was planted, but time and lime have made it amenable. Even now very deep planting is necessary, as the top soil dries off very rapidly in hot weather. Lilies of various kinds, especially Lilium auratum, speciosum, monadelphum and the Canadian varieties, do very well, while every sort of campanula flourishes exceedingly. Those charming bulbs that we owe to South Africa, ixias and sparaxis, with the hardy calochorti from North America, stand the winter well by being covered with a little bracken, which preserves them sufficiently from frosts. The Californian poppywort, delicate alike in the texture of its flowers and its fragrance, adds its stately beauty and spreads freely underground, but Asclepias tuberosa (better called Butterfly Silkweed) point blank refuses to grow despite the sandy soil which text-books preach for it. Needless to say, before roses could be induced to make their home here, no little clay was imported, but, that done, they grow well, and delphiniums, in common with most herbaceous things, add the charms of their serried spikes in blues from lavender to indigo. Though Mr. Bidlake is skilful more than common with his planting, the garden owes

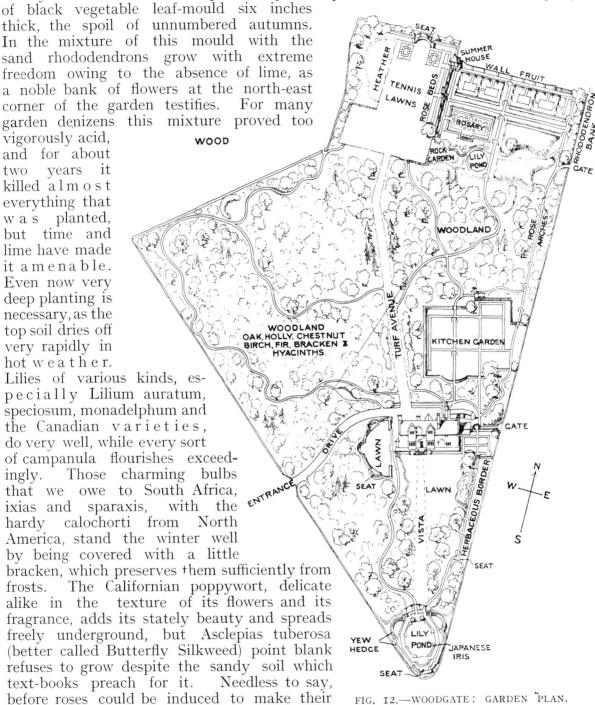

FIG. 12.—WOODGATE: GARDEN PLAN.

FIG. 13.—POOL IN WATER GARDEN.

no less to design, and the more so because it seems to have come about so naturally. In this connection one cannot agree with Emerson, whose pronouncements on matters æsthetic must always be approached with some suspicion. " Our arts," he says, " are happy hits. We are like the musician on the lake, whose melody is sweeter than he knows." This would serve well as a polite apologia for the effect of accidental charm which can bear no close examination, but is misleading nonsense when considered. Whatever may be the merits of impressionism in painting, post or otherwise, it is a snare in architecture and in the daughter art of garden design. The truth is to be sought rather in the cogent phrases of Mr. Reginald Blomfield, when he said " There is no such thing as impressionism in architecture. Our art does not allow us to leave our conception sketched out. The idea must be thought out to the uttermost. The incomplete phrase, in our case, is no

FIG. 14.—WOODGATE : A LILY POND.

phrase at all, and as far as it goes, our expression must be at least equal to our thought." The feeling that Woodgate inspires in its garden setting is that the thought has been careful and sustained, and the expression adequate. If the plan be examined, and it is worth careful study, it is clear that the clearing for the house was made in just the right spot. It affords a drive from the western road just long enough to give a pleasurable sense of anticipation, while it gives a short access for tradesmen from the eastern road. South of the house enough woodland was cleared to give an adequate lawn, surrounded by a belt of oaks through which there is a vista towards the small formal garden, occupying the southern angle of the site. Here is placed a large lily pond with Japanese iris at its corners, surrounded by a yew hedge. A small lawn has also been made on the west side of the house to prevent the undue darkening by overshadowing trees of the drawing-room bay window. East of the house is another little garden on geometrical lines, and in general the terrace and steps on the south front do homage to that element of formality which is the essence of good gardening near a house. As we leave from the building that quality dies away and the design is determined by the position of the big oaks and other trees which it was so desirable to retain. Northwards the garden has been subtly incorporated with the woodland that shelters the house from the cold winds, and the four acres covered by trees are threaded by many winding walks which lead us through a carpet of hyacinth and fern at their several seasons. It may be suggested that it would have been better to have laid down these paths on straighter and more formal lines. The intention was to create the feeling of those woodland paths that take their random windings from the feet of children, who follow the line of least resistance and walk where Nature has been less prodigal of growth. From the house porch there is a long avenue, straight save for one break, which hides the far garden until it bursts into view. After the shadow of the wood the sunlit lawn comes with that quality of surprise which is so valuable in garden design. The avenue leads past a well-equipped kitchen garden on the right to the spacious tennis lawns and bowling green fringed at the north corner by a bank of purple heather, and free of the shade of the trees. From this upper garden a long flight of brick steps takes us down to another, six feet below. A retaining wall with pillars flanking the stairway divides the two, and at its north end is a tall two-storeyed summer-house which serves both levels, as a retiring-place for tea above, and as a house for garden tools below.

In this lower garden is a maze of formal walks separated by clipped beech hedges, crossed by rose arches luxuriantly clad and bordered by beds of herbaceous flowers. South of the rosery are a rock garden and a little lily pond, where the great white blooms of gladstoniana stand free above the water boldly until the autumn frosts, and red masses of gloriosa float fragrantly. Near by is a little place consecrated to spring bulbs. A good feature of the garden is the judicious use of seats, which are placed at all points of vantage, such as the upper lawn, the rose and rock gardens, the end of the herbaceous walk, etc.

The grounds at High Coxlease, Lyndhurst, are laid out with less wealth of detail, but are none the less a highly interesting example of a garden stolen from the wild. It would be difficult to find a more enticing site for a house than this little clearing in the heart of the New Forest. One used as a child to picture just such a setting for the cottage of Jacob Armitage, the pious old verderer in " The Children of the New Forest." Though High Coxlease is so near the town of Lyndhurst, it has the atmosphere of remoteness. It would not be surprising to meet there young Edward Beverly, the excellent prig of Marryat's story, answering that question which always

FIG. 15.—HIGH COXLEASE : ENTRANCE FRONT.

FIG. 16.—THE SOUTH SIDE.

enchanted at least one eager boy, " Can you tell the slot of a brocket from a stag ? "
Obviously it is the place for brockets. If, however, we must stand upon the letter
of the law, High Coxlease, though in the world of the New Forest, is not of it. It is
the freehold of the Crown, and leased to the owner of the house which the illustrations
show embowered in its trees, but it has nothing to do with the true forest land. The
planting of High Coxlease is also modern, as the forest goes, for it was done with the
rest of the property somewhere about 1830. The plantation was made to some
purpose, for it has a finely mature aspect, and no more clearing was allowed than

seemed absolutely needful for
house and garden. The picture
of the entrance front shows
the drive fringed with bracken
and the roof framed in foliage,
and, indeed, it is impossible
to make anything like a
general survey of the house
save through a foreground
broken by trees. This setting
of the wild has been respected
in a wise spirit. As the
ground slopes southward the
lawn is bounded by a retaining
wall, beyond which a delightful
rock and water garden has
been made. The water itself
makes a home for many of
the beautiful hybrid water-
lilies evolved by the genius
of M. Latour Marliac. The
introduction of these dainty
flowers, embracing as they
do a wide range of colours,
has completely revolutionised
the art of water-gardening
in this country, and has
given it fresh scope and
purpose. The accompanying
picture shows how well they
thrive at Lyndhurst. In the
rather flat rock garden which
frames the pool, choice examples of interesting saxifrages

FIG. 17.—IN THE ROCK AND WATER GARDEN.

with encrusted leaves find a congenial place, and their silvery foliage makes
an attractive feature during those winter months when other plants are at
their worst. Many another pilgrim from the Upper Alps flourishes in this
rockery, while elsewhere in the garden some rare sorts of daphne are
obviously favourites. Such surroundings demand a house which has simplicity for
its dominant note, and no less can be said of the building which Professor Lethaby
set there in 1901. Plain white walls and chimneys, red roofs, a lead-covered porch
of curiously interesting shape, and gables of moderate pitch—these are elements always

satisfying if rightly disposed. We leave High Coxlease with a glance at the garden flowers growing out of a sea of fern, the latter always beautiful, whether in its tender green of spring, its duller hue at midsummer, or its rich and rusty brown in winter, but most of all when the coming of the frost touches the green to brilliant yellow and Nature carpets the forest with an undergrowth of gold.

The especial charm of making a flower garden in a forest clearing is that the wilful tribes of Nature can be absorbed into the new population, where they will still flaunt their wild and brilliant graces. In such gardens the outlying parts are likely never to be more brilliant than in autumn, when the gold of the furze is glittering everywhere among the darker hues of heather and the fading greens of bracken. Furze is a great ally to the garden colourist, for the large and early varieties are followed by others that are small and late. As the old and pleasant saying runs, gorse is out of bloom only when kissing's out of fashion.

FIG. 18.—LILIES AND GABLES AT HIGH COXLEASE.

CHAPTER III.—A GARDEN IN BERKSHIRE.

Roses Grown as " Fountains "—Brick Dry-walling—Stone-edged Water Garden—Refined Detail and Ornaments.

ON the outskirts of the village, a high old wall, with massive buttresses and well-wrought coping, encloses a beautiful new house of moderate size, designed by Mr. Lutyens, and a piece of ground of something under three acres. The land, when taken in hand, was old garden and orchard, with a strong westerly slope ; the soil a rich loam of calcareous character. The lower part had been the apple orchard, but the greater number of the trees were dead, and many of the remainder so much crippled that but little compunction stood in the way of the removal of a certain number to make way for the new garden design.

The house is approached directly by a door in the wall to the road ; an arched passage and a paved court with a fountain leading to the main entrance. Another doorway, close to the eastern angle, leads straight into the garden by way of a paved, rose-covered pergola. Between this and the house is a small rose garden. The path is now intersected by the wider terrace running parallel with the south face of the house ; but proceeding in the original direction the paved path leads to a further

FIG. 19.—THE GARLAND ROSE. POINT OF VIEW " B " ON GENERAL PLAN (FIG. 20).

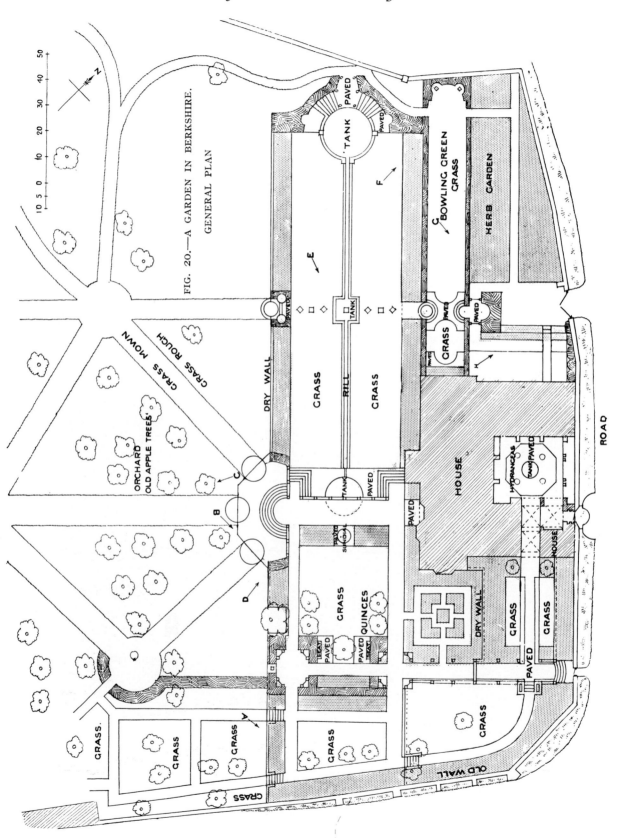

FIG. 20.—A GARDEN IN BERKSHIRE.
GENERAL PLAN

FIG. 21.—THE TANK GARDEN. POINT OF VIEW "E" ON GENERAL PLAN (FIG. 20).

display of roses; for, where
it descends by a flight of
seven steps to the orchard-
level, there are masses of
the beautiful garland rose
planted in the border above
the retaining wall. They
grow untrained in their
own way, like natural

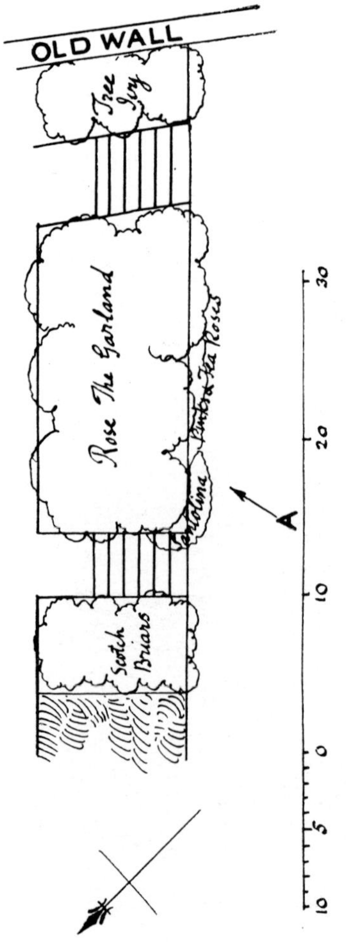

FIG. 22.—PLANTING PLAN. SEE
"A" ON GENERAL PLAN (FIG. 20)
AND PHOTOGRAPH (FIG. 25).

fountains. After rising for
six or seven feet they arch
over, and the masses of
warm white blossoms hang
down over the wall face
to within a foot or so of
the orchard-level. Some of
the old apple trees, either

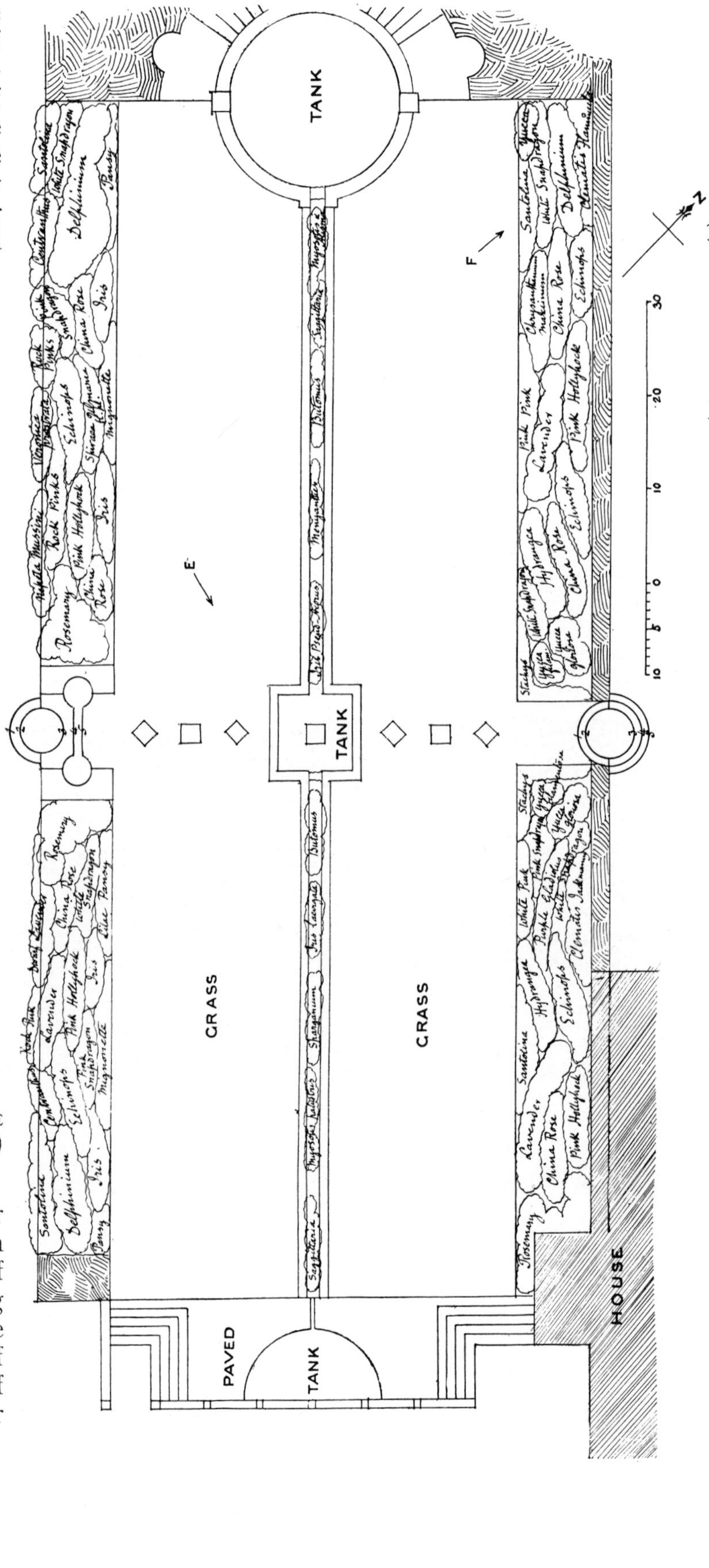

FIG. 23.—PLANTING PLAN OF TANK GARDEN. FOR PHOTOGRAPHS SEE FIG. 21 (E) AND FIG. 24 (F).

dead stumps or with only a little life in them, serve as supports for rambling roses, showing one of the several ways in which they grow willingly and display their beauty.

The locality having no stone suited for dry walling, the retaining walls of the different levels are built in brick with earth-joints for planting. In these, pinks and saxifrages, stonecrops, sandworts, rock-cresses and other small plants of mountain origin luxuriate, and, having been planted by a master hand, fall into groups of pleasant form that give enough at a time of one kind of interest. The old boundary wall, which was found covered with grass and weeds, was cleared of all undesirable growths and planted with wallflowers, Cheddar pinks, stonecrops and a few other such plants.

From a garden door in the middle of the house front a wide paved walk, joining with and crossing the terrace parallel with the house, leads straight forward to the

FIG. 24.—WEST END OF FLOWER BORDER. SEE " F " ON PLANTING PLAN (FIG. 23).

orchard, to which it descends by a bold flight of semi-circular steps on to a grassy platform following the same form. From this, three broad grass paths diverge into the orchard; the paths proceeding to certain points from which others again radiate. These grass paths, ten feet wide, are kept mown. In the spaces between, where the grass is let grow as it will, hosts of daffodils appear in spring, followed by fritillaries and meadow saffron in their seasons.

The water garden on the lower level of the house-front, reached by two angular flights of steps, is a long parallelogram. At each end is a circular tank, with a square one in the middle. They are finished with a flat stone kerb and connected in a straight line by a narrow sill having the same kerbing. It is a happy home for

FIG. 25.—THE GARLAND ROSE, HANGING OVER A DRY WALL. SEE " A " ON GENERAL PLAN (FIG. 20) AND ON PLANTING PLAN (FIG. 22).

FIG. 26.—STEPS AND DRY WALLING. VIEW POINT "D" ON GENERAL PLAN (FIG. 20).

FIG. 27.—PLANTED DRY WALL. VIEW POINT "G" ON GENERAL PLAN (FIG. 20) AND ON PLANTING PLAN (FIG. 31).

FIG. 28.—RAMBLING ROSE IN OLD APPLE. VIEW POINT "C" ON GENERAL PLAN (FIG. 20).

---

some good water-plants, the greater number of them being natives. On river banks and in the shallow waters of marshy places we often pass these good plants by with but scant notice because they are so closely pressed by masses of other less interesting vegetation ; but, brought into the garden, one is better able to appreciate their rare beauty. The water forget-me-not we all know, but the fine leaves and spreading lace-like flowers of the water plantain (*Alisma plantago*) and the almost tropical quality of the bloom of the flowering rush

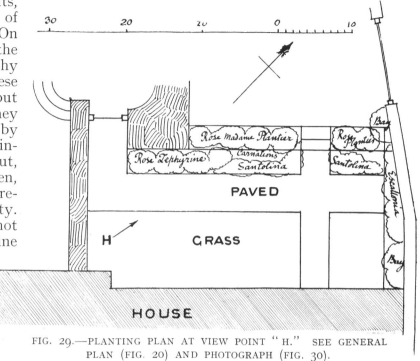

FIG. 29.—PLANTING PLAN AT VIEW POINT "H." SEE GENERAL PLAN (FIG. 20) AND PHOTOGRAPH (FIG. 30).

FIG. 30.—FLOWER BORDER NEAR BACK GATE. VIEW POINT "H" ON GENERAL PLAN (FIG. 20) AND PLANTING PLAN (FIG. 29).

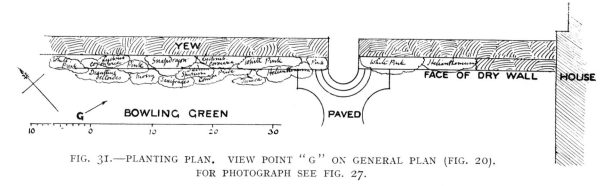

YEW

White Pink | Lychnis coronaria | Pink | Snapdragon | Lychnis coronaria | White Pink | Pink | Helianthemum

Dianthus deltoides | Thrift | Saxifrages | Shirley Loudon Pink | Tunica

White Pink | Helianthemum

FACE OF DRY WALL | HOUSE

BOWLING GREEN | PAVED

G

10   0   10   20   30

FIG. 31.—PLANTING PLAN.   VIEW POINT "G" ON GENERAL PLAN (FIG. 20).
FOR PHOTOGRAPH SEE FIG. 27.

(*Butomus umbellatus*) require the comparative isolation of some such garden culture to show their value.   The water garden is bounded on its two long sides by wide flower borders filled with a restricted choice of plants that is varied in some degree from year to year but retains certain general features.

The garden is rich in delightful detail, notably some remarkably refined figures in bronze and stone ; one in the entrance court fountain, another on a pedestal in the square tank of the water garden, and a bronze Mercury at the southern end of the detached octagonal pergola.   The paved paths, with their several flights of steps of varied and always pure design, add greatly to refinement and also to a comfortable impression of permanence in this remarkably beautiful and charming garden.

CHAPTER IV.—WESTBROOK, GODALMING.

Situation—Special Compartments—Careful Planting Scheme—Winter Garden—Covered Seats—Flower Border Facing North.

WHEN an architect of ripe experience and keen sensibility plans a house and garden for his own home, one may look for something more than usually interesting, and in Westbrook one is not disappointed. The house, built by Mr. Thackeray Turner of the hard local sandstone, stands on a plateau of high ground to the west of Godalming ; the deep valley of the river Wey is to the north and the valley of a tributary stream a little way to the south. The upper trees of a steep hanger on the northern side rise protectingly, and on all the outskirts there are also trees, with here and there a distant view between their masses.

The garden fronts are nearly south and west. On the south side a low wall encloses a paved space with beds and border of flowers, an eastward flight of steps leading down to further flower-borders. Straight in front is a wide, quiet lawn, bounded on the right by a long paved path shaded by pleached limes.

The garden to the west of the house abounds in charming surprises. Its various subdivisions are linked together in a simple general design. Each section shows some distinct way of making a garden picture, and each entices onwards to the next by the charm of mystery and the stimulus of pleasant anticipation of something still better to follow. The main design has a walling of yew hedges, now, after a growth of thirteen years, approaching maturity. Within their several compartments are a small sunk garden of summer flowers, a rose garden and one for late autumn. Between these, crossing and forming in both directions the axis of the design, are twelve-foot-wide grass paths with flower-borders on either hand ; the bright blossom showing finely against the background of dark yew. Turning southward at the intersection of the two grassy ways, a double arch of yew comes in

FIG. 32.—THE PLEACHED LIME WALK, FROM THE STUDY WINDOW. VIEW POINT " B " ON GENERAL PLAN (FIG. 33).

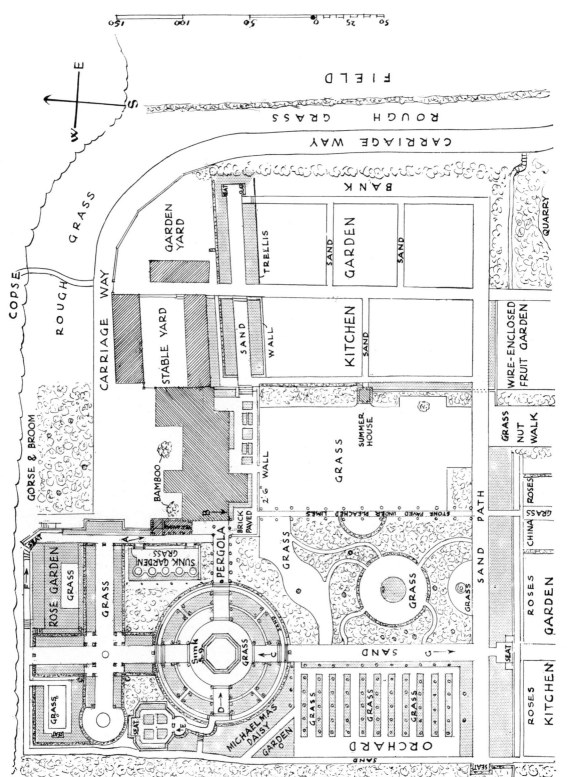

FIG. 33.—WESTBROOK : GENERAL PLAN OF GARDEN.

sight. Through and beyond this is the principal feature of the design, a large circular sunk garden for flowers of the middle and later year—an amphitheatre of summer glory (Figs. 36 to 38). Four ways, twelve feet wide, with groups of steps and partly sloping, lead to the lower grassy level, where a large octagonal tank with a wide stone kerb has groups of many coloured water-lilies. The four ways are punctuated, just within

FIG. 34.—A ROOFED SEAT.

the borders, by evergreens of upright habit, Chinese junipers, golden junipers and Irish yews. Looking from the western side, the garden takes its place as an adjunct to the house, with which it is connected by a pergola. Looking north and south there is the double yew arch with the further green paths and borderings of flower and shrub. The scheme of planting of the circular garden is interesting and effective. The sections

FIG. 35.—THE LOGGIA. VIEW POINT "A" ON PLAN (FIG. 33).

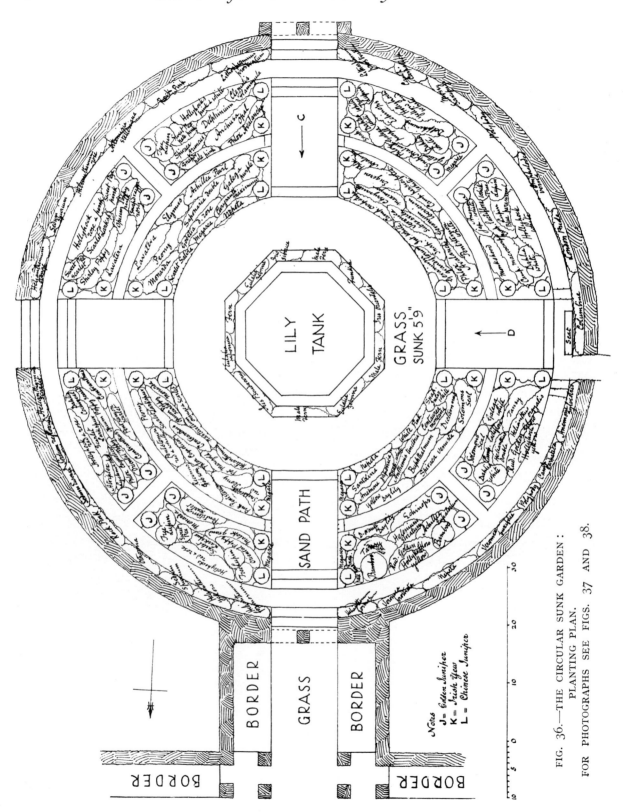

FIG. 36.—THE CIRCULAR SUNK GARDEN: PLANTING PLAN.
FOR PHOTOGRAPHS SEE FIGS. 37 AND 38.

that are in full blaze of the noonday and early afternoon sun are of strong, warm colouring, for the most part orange and scarlet ; the colour-scheme working round both ways to the cool and tender tints that are more acceptable on the shadier sides. The plan, reproduced in Fig. 36, gives an idea of the general arrangement, lesser details being omitted.

Going southward from this garden there is again the broad path, but of the local sand, which binds well ; here there is an orchard of apples, pears and plums on the right, and a thick shrubbery to the left. Concealed in the middle of the shrubbery

FIG. 37.—THE SUNK GARDEN FROM THE SOUTH. VIEW POINT " C " ON GENERAL PLAN (FIG. 33) AND PLANTING PLAN (FIG. 36).

is a fifty-foot circle of grass with a bed of heaths in the centre—a pleasantly secluded retreat. Five winding paths lead out of it through the shrubs and trees in different directions, giving access to various points, and also serving as unobtrusive means of escape when a tired worker desiring rest and solitude becomes aware of approaching intrusion.

From the western upper side of the circular garden a narrow path leads out, and, turning to the right, goes—whither ? Another slight turn, between dry-walling to right and left, reveals a solid double arch of stone leading into an enclosed space about thirty-five feet each way (Fig. 40). It is the winter garden—a delightful invention !

FIG. 38.—THE SUNK GARDEN, FROM THE WEST. VIEW POINT "D" ON GENERAL PLAN (FIG. 33) AND PLANTING PLAN (FIG. 36).

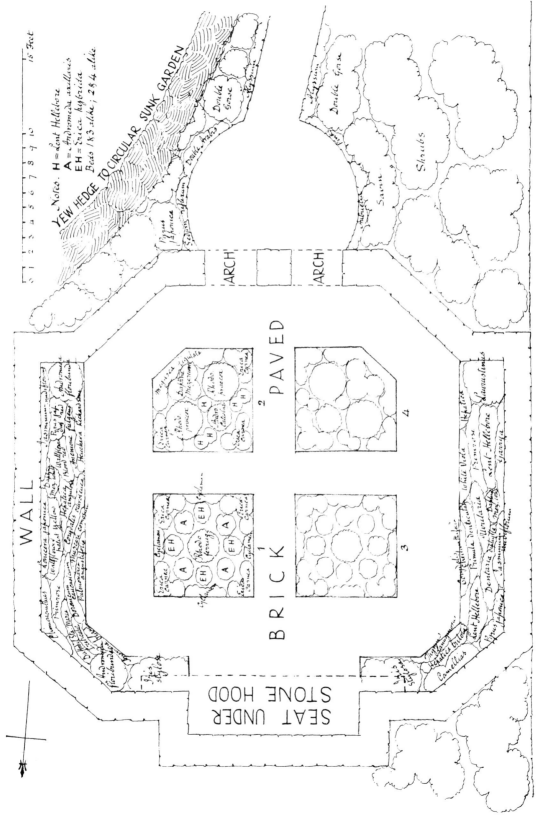

FIG. 39.—THE WINTER GARDEN: PLANTING PLAN.

Walled on all sides, the walling not high enough to exclude the low winter sun, it is absolutely sheltered.   Four beds are filled with heaths, daphne, Rhododendron præcox and a few other plants.   These beds, in company with the surrounding borders and the well-planted wall joints, show a full clothing of plants and a fair proportion of bloom from November to April (for planting plan, see Fig. 39).   The brick-paved

FIG. 40.—THE WINTER GARDEN.   VIEW POINT " E " ON GENERAL PLAN (FIG. 33).

FIG. 41.—A SHELTERED SEAT.

paths are always dry, and a seat in a hooded recess is a veritable sun-trap. The garden is rich in such sheltered seats, built and roofed, for, besides this one in the winter garden, and the loggia adjoining the house, there are two others at distinctive points (Figs. 34 and 41). They are important in the garden design in addition to their practical purpose ; moreover, even if in passing by they are not actually used, it is a comfort to the eye and mind both to see the well-designed structure bounding some garden picture and to know of the comfortable and refreshing refuge. There is an important summer-house on the eastern side of the lawn, with solid stone walls and a tiled roof. It is cool all day, for a slight air passes through, and the doorways, facing east and west, only admit the earliest and latest sun.

The experiment of placing one of the most important flower-borders on the north side of a high wall has answered admirably. The light soil of the garden soon dries up, and in all but the wettest summers the plants have evidently been benefited by the protection from hot sunshine at the root.

The pleached lime walk (Fig. 32) leads straight to a pretty place in the further garden, a long, straight walk of turf bordered by masses of China roses and grey foliage. The further end abuts upon a field gate to a lane which is a public foot-path. It was a kindly thought of Mr. Turner to leave this in full view of passers-by, who thankfully lean their arms upon the gate and enjoy the feast of roses.

CHAPTER V.—A GARDEN IN WEST SURREY.

Poor Soil—No Definite Plan—Paved Court with Tank and Steps—Colour in Flower-borders—Woodland Paths—Thunder-house.

FIFTEEN acres of the poorest possible soil, sloping a little down towards the north, in the Surrey hills. A thin skin of peaty earth on the upper part, with a natural growth of heath, whortleberry and bracken, where a wood of Scotch fir had been cut some twelve years before ; the middle part a chestnut plantation, the lower, a poor, sandy field with a hard plough-bed about eight inches down. These were the conditions that had to be considered and adapted as well as might be to the making of a garden. In the upper, heathy part, seedlings of many kinds of trees were springing up, now fair-sized examples of twenty-five years' growth. As time went on they had to be severely thinned and at the same time thrown into carefully-considered groups, one kind of tree at a time being given pre-eminence. A clearing in the chestnut copse gave space for the future lawn, house and near garden. The lower ground was deeply trenched and heavily manured for many years, and is now a productive kitchen garden. Much of the ground had to be laid out, in some kind of way, before it was known where the house was to stand, with the result that there are portions that meet at awkward angles. In fact, there was no definite planning at the beginning. Various parts were taken in hand at different times and treated on their individual merits, and the whole afterwards reconciled as might most suitably be contrived. The only portion with a definite plan is a small paved court between two wings of the house and a double flight of steps enclosing a tank, all forming one

FIG. 42.—THE TANK AND STEPS. VIEW POINT " B " ON GENERAL PLAN (FIG. 44).

FIG. 43.—THE PAVED COURT AND STEPS. VIEW POINT 6 YARDS BACK FROM "A" ON GENERAL PLAN (FIG. 44) THIS PHOTOGRAPH WAS TAKEN IN 1908. COMPARE WITH FIG. 45, WHICH SHOWS GROWTH OF CLEMATIS MONTANA IN 1912. AND WITH FIG. 42, WHICH SHOWS PRESENT STAGE OF CLIPPED BOX BALLS.

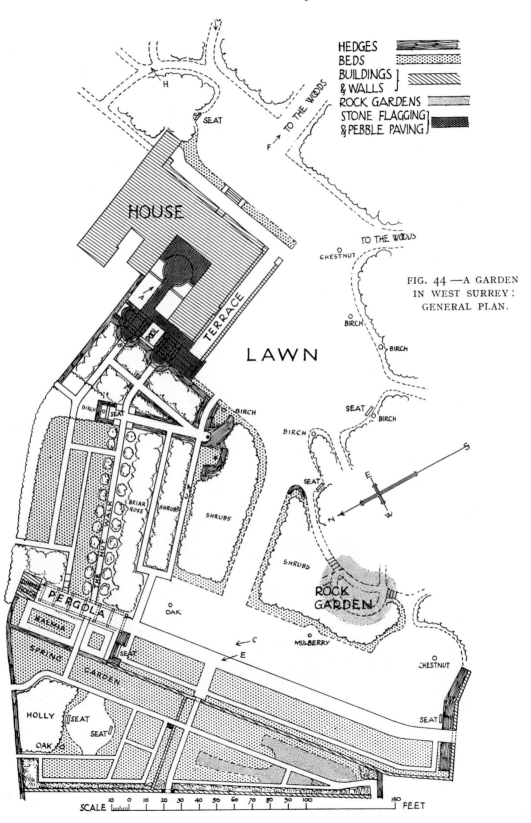

FIG. 44 — A GARDEN
IN WEST SURREY:
GENERAL PLAN.

FIG. 45.—THE PAVED COURT. VIEW POINT "A" ON GENERAL PLAN (FIG. 44).

FIG. 46.—THE EAST END OF THE MAIN FLOWER-BORDER. VIEW POINT "C" ON GENERAL PLAN (FIG. 44).

FIG. 47.---YUCCAS IN THE FLOWER-BORDER.   VIEW POINT "E" ON GENERAL PLAN
(FIG. 44).

FIG. 48.—A SPECIAL BORDER OF GREY, WHITE, PINK AND PURPLE.
(SEE FIG. 49 FOR PLANTING PLAN.)

FIG. 49.—A SPECIAL BORDER OF GREY, WHITE, PINK AND PURPLE.
(FOR PHOTOGRAPH SEE FIG. 48.)

design (Figs. 43 and 45). The court has a circular pavement, partly between two box-edged beds and partly bounded by a raised step next the house. On the sides of the raised pavement stand pots of fern and funkia, forming a good green setting for potted plants in flower---lilies, bellflowers, hydrangeas, etc., according

FIG. 50.—THE GREEN WOOD-WALK. VIEW POINT "F" ON GENERAL PLAN (FIG. 44).

to their season.   Clematis montana drapes one side wall and hangs as a garland from the lower moulded beam of the timber-framed overhang.   The opposite wall is clothed with a vine.   The stairways on each side of the tank are punctuated by eight balls of clipped box.   The tank itself has a wealth of ferns growing out of its cool, north-facing wall, the water being let in by a finely-designed lion mask, the work of Mr. G. D. Leslie, R.A. (Fig. 42).

From the lawn a wide turfway leads to another at right angles, beyond which is the main border of hardy flowers, eighteen feet wide and about one hundred and eighty feet long (Fig. 46).   It is backed by a narrow alley, not seen from the front, but serving conveniently to get at the plants in the back of the border, and those on the other side against a high wall of the local hard sandstone.   The border has a definite colour scheme ; at the two ends blue, white and palest yellow, with grey foliage ; and purple, white and pink, also with grey foliage, respectively ; the colour then advancing from both ends by yellow and orange, to the middle glory of strongest reds. Bold groups of yucca are at the ends, and flank a cross-path that passes by a doorway through the wall (Fig. 47). A plan of the actual planting, and details of some uncommon ways of utilising some of the plants to gain unusual advantages, are given in Miss Jekyll's book, " Colour Schemes in the Flower Garden." A special border in the further part of the garden is given entirely to a colour scheme of purple, white and pink, with grey foliage (Figs. 48 and 49). It follows, from there having been no exact design for the whole, that the garden falls into separate spaces—an accident that has been used to some advantage by devoting each space to a season.

FIG. 51.—ONE OF THE WAYS FROM WOOD TO LAWN.
VIEW POINT "G" ON GENERAL PLAN (FIG. 44).

The woodland closely adjoins the lawn and garden ground, and much care has been given to the regions where the one melts into the other.   From a narrow lawn that is next to the south front of the house a wide grassy way runs straight up into the wood, to a point where, at some distance away, a fine old Scotch fir, double-stemmed and therefore spared when the rest of the wood was cut, ends the view, which is still

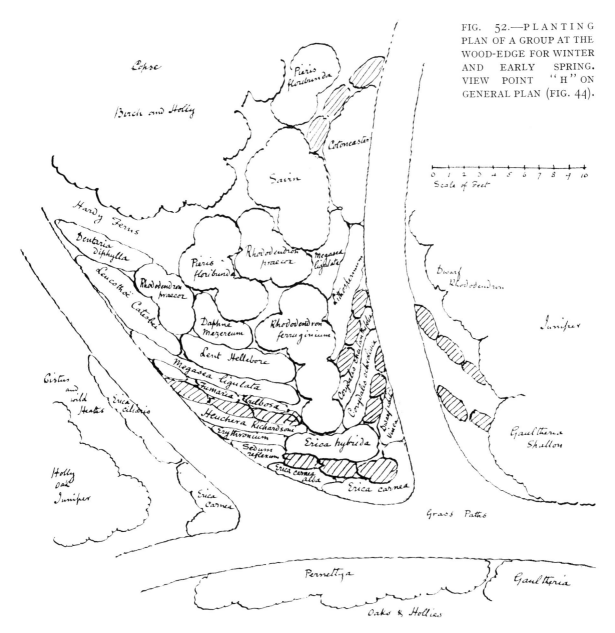

FIG. 52.—PLANTING PLAN OF A GROUP AT THE WOOD-EDGE FOR WINTER AND EARLY SPRING. VIEW POINT "H" ON GENERAL PLAN (FIG. 44).

backed by more distant wood. This wide green walk (Fig. 50) is the most precious possession of the place, the bluish distance giving a sense of some extent and the bounding woodland one of repose and security, while in slightly misty weather the illusions of distance and mystery are endless and full of charm. Nearest the lawn are groups of rhododendron, very carefully chosen for colour, with hardy ferns and one of the smaller andromedas filling up nearest the grass on the shady side, and tufts of the natural wild heaths, intergrown with the blue-flowered Lithospermum prostratum, on the side where the sun shines for some hours of the day.

Of the lesser grassy ways into the wooded ground, one that passes under the shade of oaks and birches has groups of some of the beautiful wild ferns—male fern, lady fern and dilated shield fern, in the natural setting of mossy ground and whortle-berry, and a complete backing of bracken, with here and there a flowery incident—a patch of trillium, and further a little bank of the lovely little trientalis and a bold back grouping of Solomon's seal and white foxglove (Fig. 51). Another passes from the lawn between banks of Gaultheria, alpenrose and the larger shrubby andromedas ; it is shown from above at Fig. 53. Another passes up through a region of azalea and cistus. The intention of all the paths from garden to wood is to lead by an imperceptible gradation from one to the other by the simplest means that may be devised, showing on the way the beauty of some one or two good kinds of plant and placing them so that they look happy and at home.

One place where two of the paths join that lead up to the wood has been arranged with a larger number of kinds of plants as a bit of garden for winter and earliest spring, but here the restful feeling is preserved by keeping the colouring within a

FIG. 53.—AUTUMN-BLOOMING SHRUBS. VIEW POINT " J " ON GENERAL PLAN (FIG. 44).

restricted range of low-toned pinks and purples, with a fair amount of quiet, deep-coloured leafage. The planting plan (Fig. 52) shows the arrangement.

There are but comparatively few shrubs that bloom in autumn ; two of them, viz., Æsculus macrostachya and Olearia Haastii, have been grouped together by one of the paths between the shrub-clumps.

At the far end of the kitchen garden, where the north and west walls join at an uneven angle, stands a little building—a raised gazebo. From inside the garden its floor-level is gained by a flight of steps that wind up with one or two turns. Its purpose is partly to give a fitting finish to a bare-looking piece of wall and partly to provide a look-out place over the fields and the distant range of chalk hill to the north ; for the region of the house and garden is so much encompassed by woodland that there is no view to the open country. The little place is most often used when there is thunder about, for watching the progress of the storm, and an incised stone on the garden side bears its name of " Thunder-house." Fig. 54 shows it as seen from the road outside. One of its four openings is blocked by weather-boarding because if left open it would have overlooked a neighbour's house and garden.

FIG. 54.—THE THUNDER-HOUSE.

CHAPTER VI.—HIGHMOUNT, GUILDFORD.

Site and Views—Excavation of Chalk—Rose Garden—Planted Walls—Garden-houses—
Colour Schemes—Framing the Views.

HIGHMOUNT is one of the new houses standing on the chalk ridge that rises immediately to the south-east of the town of Guildford. The ridge seems to stand clear up into the sky, open to all the winds of heaven. The views, embracing some of the finest points in West Surrey, are extremely extensive, and, with the exception of one short section, are panoramic for more than three-fifths of the horizon's circle. Eastward is St. Martha's Hill, church-crowned ; the horizon is then cut by the bold promontory of the Chantry Woods on a spur of sandy hill. The view then opens to its full extent, passing over the southern portion of Surrey, then over the whole width of the wooded Weald of Sussex, to the dim, far line of the South Downs. A little way to the west are the fine outlines of Blackdown and Hindhead,

FIG. 55.—CIRCULAR TANK AND STEPS AT WEST END OF ROSE GARDEN.   POINT OF VIEW "A" ON
GENERAL PLAN (FIG. 56).

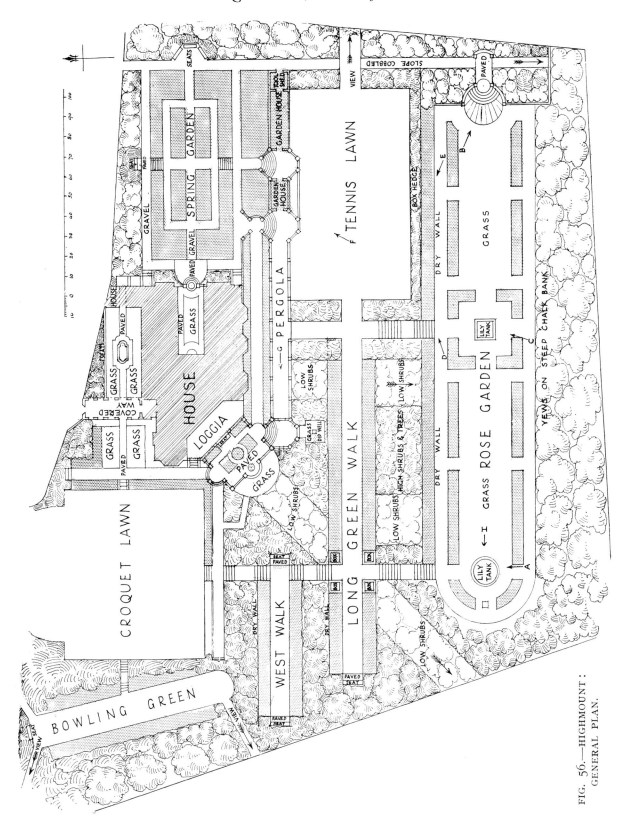

FIG. 56.—HIGHMOUNT:
GENERAL PLAN.

about fourteen miles away. Still more to the right Wolmer Forest appears as a bluish haze; nearer in the same direction are the woods in the region of Waverley Abbey, and, close at hand, the valley of the Wey, backed by the ruined Chapel of St. Catherine on its steep hill of sand and rock.

The garden ground, all on the southern face of the hill, but so near the top that it is greatly exposed, had already been laid out to a certain degree when the garden designer took it in hand. Tennis lawn, croquet lawn and bowling green had been levelled and made; but the steepness of the remainder, composed of grassy slopes between clumps of shrubs and flowers of no particular design, was found to be incommodious, and great need was felt for

FIG. 57.—STEPS AND PAVEMENT AT THE EAST END OF ROSE GARDEN. VIEW POINT "B" ON GENERAL PLAN (FIG. 56).

something more restful and systematic. It was evident that nothing satisfactory could be done without a serious amount of moving of earth. The ground lay in humps and hollows too blunt and shapeless in form to be utilised as they were, and yet with sides so steep that foothold was precarious and all progression uncomfortable. Happily, the owners were willing to face the necessary outlay, by no means a slight one; for digging in pure chalk is almost as serious a matter as quarrying in stone, and in places it was necessary to go eight feet into the solid, and also to find means of disposal of the waste stuff excavated. This was tipped all along the lowest of the ground to form a firm embankment for the rose garden. It was found just possible to get a width of fifty-five feet and a length of two hundred and eighty feet, so that

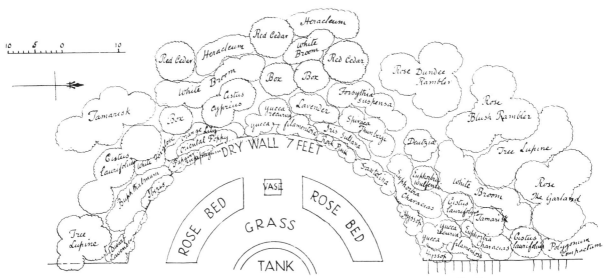

FIG. 58.--PLANTING PLAN OF TOP OF CIRCULAR DRY WALL. VIEW POINT "H" ON GENERAL PLAN (FIG. 56).

FIG. 59.--FROM THE MIDDLE OF THE ROSE GARDEN. VIEW POINT "C" ON GENERAL PLAN (FIG. 56).

there should be the comfort of a space fairly large and quite level, where there had formerly been a kind of nightmare of confused and treacherous declivities. Therefore, with ground rising on all sides but the south, the whole rose garden appears to be sunk, the additional comfort being acquired of absolute shelter from the north and of lying open to the sun. At the western end a bold segmental

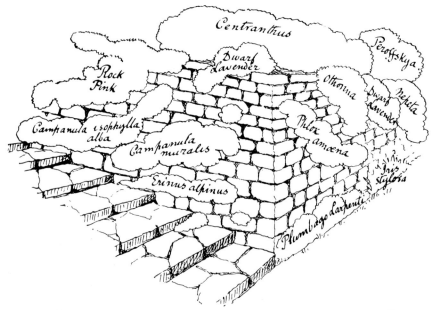

FIG. 60.—SKETCH OF PLANTING AS SEEN FROM VIEW POINT "D" ON GENERAL PLAN (FIG. 56).

FIG. 61.—ANGLE OF DRY WALL FROM VIEW POINT "D" ON GENERAL PLAN (FIG. 56).

curve of high retaining wall also gives shelter from any wind coming from a westerly direction. As will be seen in the general plan (Fig. 56), this encloses a lily tank and encircling rose-beds (Fig. 55); the rose-beds are continued as straight borders on either side along the whole length; the quiet middle green space is broken only by the square tank midway of the whole (Fig. 59). The eastern end has a flight of circular steps with a bold half-round paving at the foot (Fig. 57). This, with the pergola, garden-houses and their accompanying flights of steps on some of the upper levels, is the work of Mr. Douglas Round. Thus the rose garden is a long, level green parallelogram, quiet and restful, where before was only tumbled and disordered futility.

FIG. 62.—CAMPANULA ISOPHYLLA ALBA, IN THE DRY WALL, FROM VIEW POINT " E " ON GENERAL PLAN (FIG. 56).

At the western end, backing the lily tank and rose-beds, the circular retaining wall is from six to seven feet high. The top is rather boldly planted with yuccas, the great Euphorbia Wulfenii, cistus, tamarisk and tree lupine, and, further back, with tree box, white broom and red cedar (Fig. 58). Barely two years planted, the whole is as yet too immature to show anything like the ultimate intention. Facing uphill across the tank one looks up a series of steps, rising flight after flight (Fig. 55). The two lowest, with a landing between, rise to a broad turf path between flower borders, running eastward to the tennis lawn and giving a long green vista of over three hundred feet, with again the feeling of reposeful space and security that had formerly been wanting. The whole length of the rose garden has its six-foot-high retaining wall planted; not planted all over, but enough to display a number of beautiful things in suitable groups, the same plants being carried up on the top of the wall, where there is a space of four feet between the wall top and the hedge of tree box that surrounds the tennis lawn at the eastern end. The same space is also between the top of the wall and the shrubs

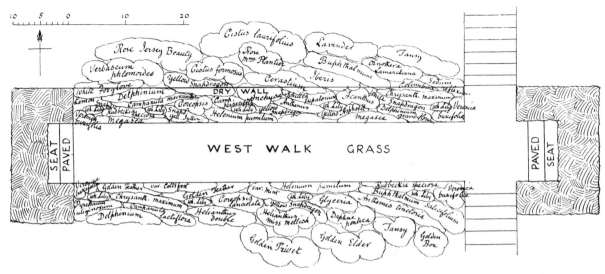

FIG. 63.—PLANTING PLAN OF BORDERS OF WEST WALK. SEE GENERAL PLAN (FIG. 56).

and bush roses that approach it further to the west. The wall is in full sun, and the good plants and sub-shrubs that we have from the Mediterranean region—lavender, rosemary, santolina, othonna and so on, with pinks, stonecrops and several of the rock-loving campanulas of the Alps (to name only a few of the plants utilised)—rejoice in the full southern exposure and the brilliant, unveiled light of the high elevation.

FIG. 64.—THE GARDEN-HOUSES, FROM VIEW POINT "F" ON GENERAL PLAN (FIG. 56).

The strong calcareous loam is also favourable, and the position in the joints between the stones, giving shelter and protection from wet to the crown of the plant, made it possible to use plants that would otherwise not be hardy. Conspicuously beautiful at Highmount, though so lately planted, is the tender South Italian Campanula isophylla, usually grown in greenhouses and not hardy in the open, though here in rampant growth and fullest health and development. Looking up the double flight of steps from the rose garden across the square tank from C (Fig. 59), a patch of this fine campanula shows on the right; the same group comes to the left of the picture in the angle view from D (Fig. 61). A further view from E shows another patch on the

FIG. 65 —THE WEST END OF THE PERGOLA, FROM VIEW POINT "G" ON GENERAL PLAN (FIG. 56).

face of the wall, with a group of nepeta (the pretty purple catmint) above and the Algerian Iris stylosa at the wall foot (Fig. 62).

The garden-houses, standing on the north side of the tennis lawn, will, in time, be pleasantly framed by the vines planted on the pergolas which bound and roof the two flights of steps giving access to the tennis lawn from the end of the main pergola and the garden above (Fig. 64). The building on the right has a nearly flat roof of corrugated iron, whose unsightliness has been veiled by a coating of earth and a planting of stone-crops. Above the buildings is the garden of spring flowers, where, besides all the other good things, it is a yearly joy to see the wonderful vigour and bloom of the wall-flowers. All the *cruciferæ* rejoice in a limy soil—stocks, wallflowers, iberis, alyssum, æthionema, with others of the same large botanical family, on such a soil are seen at their best.   The flower borders are carefully considered for colour arrangement ; the long green walk has a massing of strong reds and yellows in the middle of the length, with the ends cooler coloured, in the way that seems to make the most satisfactory colour picture.   A shorter upper double border, called the west walk, is mostly of yellows, with tender and brilliant blue (Fig. 63).   These colour-schemes are not only highly satisfactory in themselves, but they serve to give individuality and a quality of dignity and distinction to various portions of a garden.   Offering to the eye one clear picture at a time, they rescue the beholder from the distracting impression of general muddle and want of distinct intention that is so frequent in gardens and so wasteful—wasteful because a place may be full of fine plants, grandly grown, but if they are mixed up without thought or definite scheme they only produce an unsatisfactory effect, instead of composing together into a harmonious picture.

Although the view at Highmount is very extensive, it is from the pictorial point of view not as beautiful as it might be, and as it is confidently hoped it will be in a few years' time.   The material is there for at least half-a-dozen beautiful scenes, but, just as a painted picture is comparatively of little effect without its frame, so in a much greater degree is the outdoor picture.   Everyone has noticed how, coming suddenly on some perhaps quite tame garden scene through a doorway, it seems to be invested with a strange kind of beauty.   So, in the case of a view that is over-panoramic, we plant so as to cut it up and frame it in different directions.   A glance at the general plan (Fig. 56) will show how this is provided for, the more deeply-shaded masses of shrubs and trees comprising such as will rise high enough to come well above the horizon line and make of each opening a definite picture.   In the plan the chief points of view so separated are shown by the feathered arrows

CHAPTER VII.—THE TREATMENT OF SMALL SITES.

Some Gardens by Mr. Inigo Triggs—The Value of Historical Examples—Paved Parterres—The Use of Treillage—A Town Garden by Mr. Lutyens—A Seaside Garden by Mr. Mallows—Planting Scheme by Mr. H. Avray Tipping—Various Typical Examples.

THERE is no problem before the architect and garden designer more difficult, and at the same time more attractive, than is presented by small sites, and particularly by the long, narrow spaces that go with houses of small frontage. So important are the limitations of the latter that a separate chapter has been devoted to the treatment of a typical case, *i.e.*, Millmead, Bramley (pages 1 to 9). In this chapter will be described various examples of successful small gardens that owe their charm mainly to skilful design, however well that has been expressed and emphasised by right choice in planting. Where the area to be dealt with is a small rectangle and flat, there are few better ways of treating it than by laying out a paved garden with or without grass, but preferably with it. If grass be omitted altogether, winter, with its empty flower-beds, brings a grim and bare look. It is fitting to begin the series with one devised by Mr. H. Inigo Triggs.

The revival of the right principles of garden design in England during the last twenty years is due to a comparatively small band of people, who by word and deed have shown the right way. The first thing necessary was to go back to such old examples as had survived the onslaughts of the "landscape" school, to publish measured drawings and photographs of them, and to analyse the qualities that make their beauty. In this necessary work Mr. Inigo Triggs has taken a leading part. His great folio volumes, *Formal Gardens in England and Scotland* and *The Art of Garden Craft in Italy,* were pioneer works that did great service. The especial need of such historical research becomes obvious when it is realised how swiftly and sometimes irrevocably the aspects of gardens change. Mr. Triggs has emphasised the fact that

FIG. 66.—LITTLE BOARHUNT, LIPHOOK.

FIG. 67.—THE SUNK GARDEN AT LITTLE BOARHUNT.

no examples are extant of the garden as it appeared in the Middle Ages. If it is desired to reconstruct its features, recourse must be made to illuminated MSS. and paintings of the period. From such sources we learn about such enchanting features as the Ladies' gardens, which usually consisted of a little square enclosure surrounded by high walls. Even when we turn to much later periods we cannot be certain that the formal gardens adjoining old houses at all faithfully represent their original form. Succeeding owners and gardeners have impressed their own ideas on the gardens under their control. It is indeed doubtful whether any garden of even so recent a period as the beginning of the eighteenth century appears to-day as it did when first made. A gazebo here or a fountain there may occupy its original place, but such elements as parterres, paths and hedges are likely to have been altered beyond recognition. The student is often impressed by the divergence between the existing condition of historic gardens and their presentment in early prints. The outlines and main divisions may be the same, but with details such as the widths of borders and paths and the placing of statues so altered as to destroy the original proportions and quality of the complete scheme. The value of Mr. Triggs' work has been enhanced by the creative ability which he brought to his labours. It follows that the gardens which he has himself devised are based on a wide knowledge of what gave to the old gardens of England their peculiar attraction. In the many houses which are the fruit of his partnership with Mr. Unsworth we do not look in vain, therefore, for scholarship and original fancy. Of these, Little Boarhunt, which is his own home, is a good example. It shows how the qualities that

FIG. 68.—LITTLE BOARHUNT: STEPS, GATE AND WALL.

make the beauty of the historic formal gardens may be reproduced in little for houses of moderate size.

Whether or not it be true that King John ran a boar from Liphook to Southsea before killing, Boarhunt has been the name of a Liphook manor since the Middle Ages. The site of the house now illustrated has been called in turn Deadman's and Fry's Farm, but Mr. Inigo Triggs did wisely in reviving so pleasant a name as Little Boarhunt. Other monarchs than John have been identified with the place, which is easy to be explained, for the old road from London to Portsmouth once passed through the garden. It is an odd commentary on the levels of roads before Macadam's day that the surface of this old highway is quite twenty feet below the surrounding ground, and now forms the bottom of a woodland dell in Mr. Triggs' garden. Common lands interspersed with patches of woodland—all that now remain of the great forest of Woolmer—stretch away from the house for many miles. It is not too fanciful to guess that the garden of Little Boarhunt was the scene of a charming incident recorded by Gilbert White in the *History of Selborne.* " As Queen Anne was journeying on the Portsmouth road, she did not think the forest of Wolmer beneath her royal regard. For she came out of the great road at Lippock, which is just by, and reposing herself on a bank smoothed for that purpose, saw with great complacency and satisfaction the whole herd of red deer brought by the keepers along the vale before

FIG. 69.—A SIMPLE BRICK-BUILT DOVECOTE.

her, consisting then of about five hundred head." Mr. Inigo Triggs has smoothed many banks in the making of his garden, but the red deer have given place to pigeons. As lately as June, 1910, Little Boarhunt was a small farmhouse of no especial merit, with a barn and yard, but no garden. All the building and the remodelling of the farmyard was done in six months ; by the spring of 1911 the garden had grown up, and it now looks old-established.

The note of gaiety is struck at the entrance. Mr. Triggs has chosen to border the drive with broad beds full of herbaceous plants, instead of with the dull shrubs that too often find a place there. The farmyard to the south of the house was excavated to make a sunk rose garden. Its retaining walls of rough stone are brilliant with saxifrages, pinks and veronica. Herbaceous borders separate the surrounding paths from the low enclosing walls, which are carried up with square stone piers supporting timbers clothed with climbing roses. Particular attention is drawn to this wall treatment, which is as delightful as it is uncommon. Further reference is made to it in Chapter X. The wall is broken at its south corner by a garden-house, inexpensively built a single brick thick, with its faces cemented. In the neighbouring wall is a small old wooden hand-gate of satisfactory construction (Fig. 68). The sunk garden itself is an admirable example of the wealth of interesting detail that can be employed in a small space without creating any feeling of overcrowding. It is divided by a little brick canal, served by rain-water collected from the roof. This rill widens at its middle into a dipping pool, of practical use in watering the garden, and from it rises a slender brick column surmounted by a little Italian figure of a boy with a fish. The four beds for standard roses are divided by narrow brick paths, set out to differing designs. Altogether the garden is as pretty as can be, and has a further pleasant feature in the brick dovecote, which comes at the end of the north enclosing wall. It must be explained that the plan of Little Boarhunt shows to the south-west a green court and pool which have not yet been made, but on pages 150 and 151 are given plan and sketch of the interesting fountain treatment which Mr. Triggs has devised for it. The area covered by the sunk and walled garden now illustrated (by a comprehensive view in Fig. 67) is only ninety feet by sixty feet, and is justly described as small.

The paved garden at Island, Steep (Fig. 71), illustrates a practical point of importance. The beds are arranged in such a way that all work on the flowers can be done from the paved paths. This is useful in the many cases where ladies do not leave pruning, etc., to the gardener, and like to do the work dryshod. In this garden the parterre is sunk about eighteen inches below the general level, and there are bands of turf above and below the retaining wall, but not among the flower-beds.

Another example of a paved parterre without grass is illustrated in Fig. 72, which shows the treatment by Mr. Baillie Scott of a forecourt at the entrance front of a house at Sevenoaks. An attractive feature of it is the raised basin in the middle, which is built in coloured tiles. Other examples of like treatment are at The Platts, Petersfield, by Mr. Inigo Triggs (Fig. 74); Combelands, Pulborough, by Professor E. S. Prior (Fig. 73); and Cray, by Mr. Maberley Smith (Fig. 75). The photograph of the last of these was taken before planting was begun, and shows the garden in all the nakedness of its unclothed masonry, but it shows the levels all the better for that. It

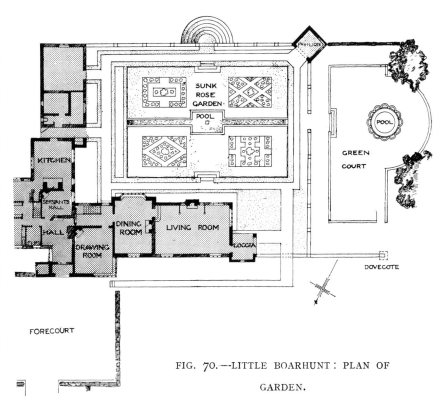

FIG. 70.—LITTLE BOARHUNT: PLAN OF

GARDEN.

should be explained that great tubs with clipped trees are intended to be placed at the ends of the tongues of paving, which otherwise would be purposeless. More detailed reference to the laying of paved work and to suitable materials are given elsewhere (Chapter XV.), but it may be noted in connection with the sunk garden at Plewland, Haslemere, designed by Messrs. Read and Macdonald (Fig. 77), that the dry-built retaining walls make, with their rough stone, a strong-looking base to the house itself. In districts where the local stone is costly for house-building or unsuitable by reason of being porous or possessing other defects, it is good to use it for garden walls. It yields a contrast with the red brick of the house and gives an impression both of roughness and stability that is helpful.

FIG. 71.—ROSE GARDEN AT ISLAND, STEEP.

In the case of small garden spaces which are overlooked there is nothing more helpful to the designer than a treillage screen. In Figs. 78 and 79 is shown a scheme, devised by Mr. Inigo Triggs, for the treatment of a square plot, which measures seventy-four feet each way. There is a stepped pool in the middle, and the shaped beds of a parterre are geometrically disposed with reference to four Irish yews. In the corners there would be wooden seats, which have been omitted in the perspective sketch for the purpose of clearness. For the same reason no roses are shown clothing the trellis and no flowers in the beds. The treillage itself is intended to be made of split oak laths interwoven basket-fashion, and the framing would also be of oak with little balls on the tops of the posts. The general effect of a scheme like this, when in being, is well shown by the photograph of a trellis garden, which is included among the illustrations of the Pergola Chapter.

Although this volume is devoted in the main to the gardens of small country houses, the designing of a town garden does not demand the application of very different principles except in so far as more conscious architectural motifs may find a just place. The garden at 100, Cheyne Walk, Chelsea, the residence of Sir Hugh

FIG. 72.—PAVED FORECOURT AT SEAL HOLLOW, SEVENOAKS.

FIG. 73.—AT COMBELANDS, PULBOROUGH.

FIG. 74.—PAVED GARDEN AT THE PLATTS, PETERSFIELD.

FIG. 75.—SUNK GARDEN AT CRAY BEFORE PLANTING.

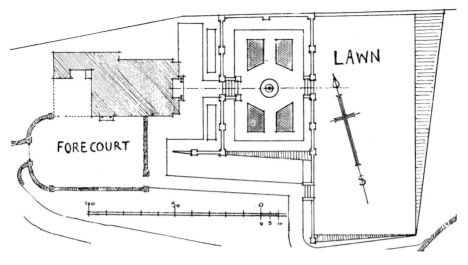

FIG. 76.—PLAN OF PLEWLAND GARDEN.

Lane, is a good example of what may be done in a limited space (Figs. 81 and 82). The garden is divided from the space at the back of the house by a simple colonnade of stone. Fortunately, there existed two fine trees, one a mulberry of noble growth, and these make brave features.

A sense of length is given to the garden by the wide parallel stone paths, the middle one of which is interrupted by a round pool. At the far end the old, uninteresting wall has been transformed by the building of two niches, which shelter statues in the classical manner. Reference to the plan (Fig. 80) shows a practical point in the provision of a narrow flagged path up the east side, which gives access to the flower-beds on either side. The whole scheme is simple and unlaboured. Too often the makers of

FIG. 77.—THE SUNK GARDEN AT PLEWLAND, HASLEMERE.

town gardens try to make up for the absence of a fine show of plants by an excess of sculpture, which raises visions of a monument mason's yard. Mr. Lutyens has shown a wise restraint, and the garden has a refined classical flavour without being stiff. When the borders are furnished at their proper seasons with such things as arabis, spreading its bloom and leafage over the paving, and later with carnations that will bring their brilliant array of colour, the garden will be complete. Carnations in particular are kindly to the town gardener, and in nowise turn against a soil that builders of many generations have salted with brick rubbish. Indeed, the lime of old mortar is often a beneficent aid.

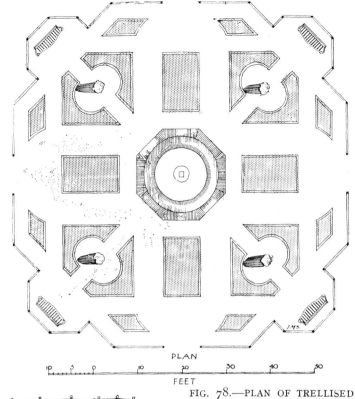

PLAN
FEET

FIG. 78.—PLAN OF TRELLISED
GARDEN.

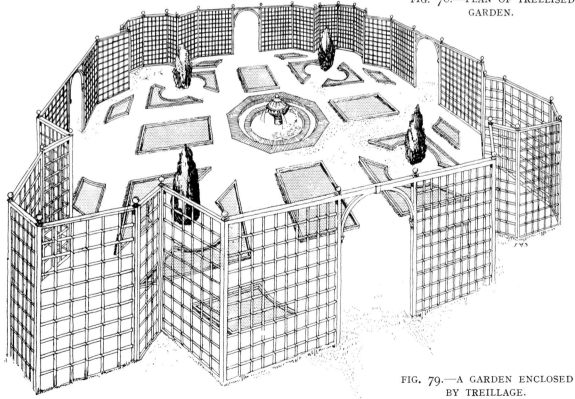

FIG. 79.—A GARDEN ENCLOSED
BY TREILLAGE.

From Chelsea to a windswept Norfolk shore is a far cry, but the conjunction is instructive, as it emphasises the great influence of wind on the design and planting of gardens. There is shown in Figs. 83 to 85 a scheme for remodelling a dilapidated little homestead at Happisburgh, designed and drawn by Mr. C. E. Mallows. The essence of the planning is the protection of the garden from the fierce and frequent winds that blow from north and east. This would be contrived by repairing an old barn on the east side to serve as a playroom or studio, and some cow hovels on the north to make a covered way, useful for summer meals or for a skittle alley. The house is on the west, and the garden is open only to the south or landward side, where additional shelter would be provided by planting trees, as described later. On the house side, a hedged recess with some sort of seat or shelter is planned so as to continue the lines of the house and form a feature and a bulwark between the flower garden and the more open lawn. The flower garden is essentially the old farmyard converted. It would be cleared out, the central part sunk and fresh soil introduced, and laid out in flagged paths and steps surrounding the flower-beds and edging the borders which lie against the buildings. The planting of such a garden would depend upon two considerations. The first is whether it is to be merely a place of summer resort, or whether it is intended for inhabitance at other seasons of the year also. The second consideration takes in the questions of soil and climate, for on some knowledge of these will largely depend the choice of plants. There are enough and to spare that will flourish here, and care should be taken in making a selection not to stray beyond this quite adequate store. The following scheme of planting has been devised by Mr. H. Avray Tipping, and will give many helpful suggestions to the owners of seaside gardens. The soil resembles that of Holland, and the Dutch have now bulb-growing competitors in East Anglia. Spring bulbs should therefore be freely used, for the sheltering buildings will save even the brittle-stalked tulip from destruction by wind.

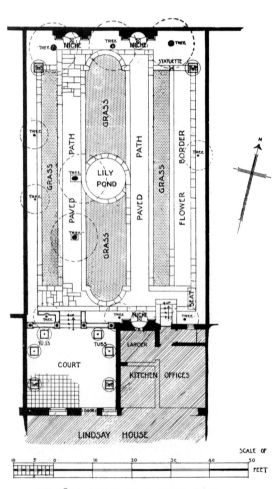

FIG. 80.—PLAN OF A TOWN GARDEN.

Short-stemmed species may be reserved to less protected areas. The formation of wind-breaks is the preliminary operation. A bank would be raised, behind which young trees can obtain early shelter. Sycamores, poplars and Austrian firs will prove the most successful. Near to the bank they should be set in serried ranks, affording mutual support, and be allowed to grow into a tangle. Further in, the planting should be more sparse, and thinning should be yearly attended to, so that the trees that are left may attain fine shape and good grouping. Where high trees are not desired, sea buckthorn will brave the gales and make a thicket. Close planting in this case also

FIG. 81.—AT 100, CHEYNE WALK, CHELSEA: POOL AND STATUES.

FIG. 82.—THE SCREEN.

FIG. 83.—SCHEME BY MR. C. E. MALLOWS FOR A SHELTERED GARDEN ON THE EAST COAST.

should be the rule, but for a further reason. Unlike our own species, that of Hippophaë rhamnoides seems to produce a majority of the male sex, and nine-tenths of them must be cut out, so that the yellow-berried Amazons of the tribe may have full scope to display their charms. Within these shelters, and even without them, the Japanese euonymus, both green and golden, will flourish, while Griselinia littoralis, Escallonia macrantha and Olearia Haastii are only a few of the other evergreens that have a friendly feeling towards the sea. But the subjects must be educated to rough usages. Let them be pot grown or yearly transplanted stuff. Plant late in spring. Use the local reed-screens against wind and sun. Be liberal with the water-pot and the syringe when the air is hot and dry. Thus treated, tamarisks, gorses and brooms will be thoroughly at home. None of these will mind a slight

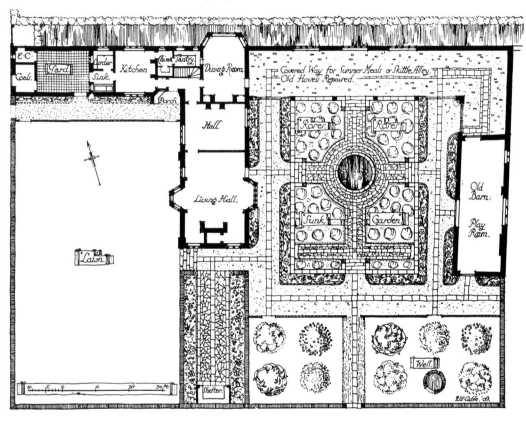

FIG. 84.—PLAN FOR A SHELTERED SEASIDE GARDEN.

sprinkle of salt or a moderate buffeting of wind, and, if rightly arranged, they will frame an enclosure as thoroughly protected as the sunk garden itself. That, with its artificial bulwarks all ready, will offer an immediate harbourage. The tree-surrounded oasis will be a future outlet for gardening energy. The early bulbs already spoken of—not tulips merely, but daffodils and hyacinths, chionodoxas and squills, anemones and crocuses—should have an accompaniment of double arabis and varied aubrietias; of wallflowers, Alpine species as well as garden hybrids; of Blue-eyed Mary and rose-coloured Himalayan primrose. The last two will share the dampest spot with some of the mossy saxifrages, while the low dry wall, which sustains the wide walks that stretch out on a level from the loggia, will be the home of the encrusted section and of sedums and houseleeks. Of the last named there are new varieties which are of a rich deep red when grown in seaside sun, and the poorest soil and driest place will suit them side by side with Zauschneria californica, which will bear its tubular scarlet blooms from July to frost. The great majority of alpines will do well here. The charm of many of them depends on their close and orderly growth and the delicate poise of their blooms. In the rich soil of enclosed and leafy valleys they are apt to take on a coarseness which renders them almost valueless. Their original deportment will, however, be well preserved in the light soil, the brisk air and the open character of the East Coast. The dry walling of the sunk garden should therefore be reserved for them, while a section of the suggested extension can be prepared for their additional location. No rockwork should be attempted. Rocks adequate in size and number to create an effect would be costly to import, and would look quite alien to the environment. But miniature hills and dales, such as we often find among sand-dunes, can be created and covered with the largest sizes of the sea-shore pebbles. Such an arrangement will exactly suit the rooting and growing habits of the plants, which will soon lay their leaves and stems over the stones. The slight acclivities may be rendered more pronounced by setting tall things on them. All the sea hollies (eryngium) would look admirable so placed. Their tough stalks withstand the wind, and that should be a consideration in making the selection. Very likely the wandflower (Sparaxis pulcherrima) might succeed here, for it will bear hard frost when

FIG. 85—POOL AND PAVING.

other conditions are favourable. Its tall wing stems, headed by the pink cascades of bloom, sway easily in wind and never break. Sea lavenders and horn poppies would be thoroughly apt, and when we seek to accentuate the depressions by planting them with lowly growths, we should not forget such seaside subjects of sessile habit as the thrifts and Silene maritima.

While there is no reason for limiting the selection to shore plants, these should be well represented, and give the note to the whole arrangement. Subjects that look awkward and unfriendly in such association should be excluded, for in the tree-girt extension which we are now considering a somewhat natural lay-out should prevail, and the formal garden alone should contain florist flowers. Of these, carnations do well, and assume their most brilliant colouring by the sea. Roses flourish if adequate shelter, such as this garden possesses, is provided. The petals of many varieties, however, become spotted and decayed by the slightest tincture of salt borne in the rain driven by a sea wind. Such should be avoided, and stout-petalled kinds chosen, such as Caroline Testout, Marie d'Orleans, Frau Karl Druschki, Belle Siebrecht and George Nabonnand. Such is a meagre outline, with only very occasional filling in, of how this bare and derelict homestead could be converted into a charming home, surrounded by flourishing gardens. In preparing a list for planting the latter, it must not be forgotten that this Cromer country has been called poppyland, and that the great tribe of poppyworts, including romneya and argemone, must be duly honoured and housed. Of shrubby growths the hardy fuchsias will flourish, while to the evergreens already mentioned Choisya ternata, lavender and rosemary must certainly be added. Probably the delightful creeping form of rosemary will here survive the winters, for it is not frost but damp which is its enemy.

We may now leave this East Coast garden of a dream, for another that is in being. In nothing is there opportunity for greater skill than in the treatment of small sites of irregular shape, such as that shown in Fig. 86. Eastwood Cottage, Walberswick, stands on a narrow tongue formed by two converging roads, and Mr. A. Winter Rose has made the most of an awkwardly-shaped plot by breaking it up into several features of interest. Two are illustrated in Figs. 87 and 88. The east corner is laid out as a rock garden, to which access is given from the sunk wall that runs along

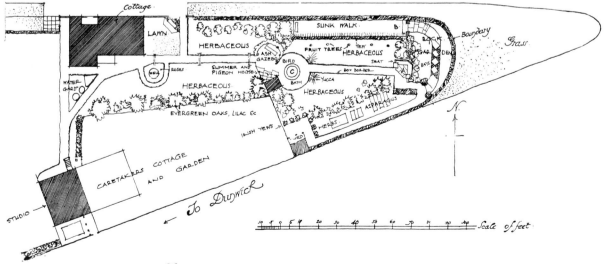

FIG. 86.—PLAN OF LITTLE GARDEN AT WALBERSWICK.

FIG. 87.—WALBERSWICK : MASONRY SEAT—   FIG. 88.—AND STEPPED PATH.

the north boundary. It is entered between a pair of masonry piers (Fig. 88), and the flagged path, broadly stepped, is in good accord with the rockwork. Its southern end is approached along a path, flanked by broad herbaceous borders, which skirts the angled seat shown in Fig. 87. Other good points about this garden are a little bird bath in the form of a circular canal and a pigeon-cote adapted from an old tool-shed.

It is not often that the laying-out of a garden suffers such interference as at Goodrich House, Hatfield, where Mr. Winter Rose had to deal with a very unusual situation. Across the length of the garden there was a right-of-way, which had to be respected, though it is rarely used. It was necessary, therefore, to divide the garden scheme into two parts. The little paved court at the back of the house is

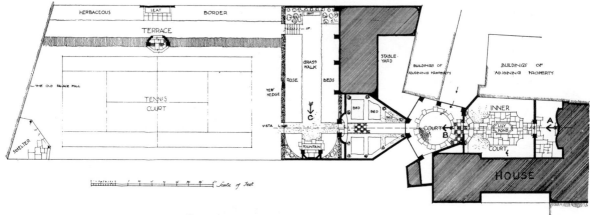

FIG. 89.—PLAN OF GARDEN AT GOODRICH HOUSE.

enclosed by two buildings, which project on each side. This section, with its charming little pool, is illustrated in Fig. 92, and the letter A on the plan (Fig. 89) shows the point of view. The right-of-way has been masked to a large extent by carrying it through a little polygonal walled space with four gateways, two on the axial line between the house and the main garden, and two on the line of the right-of-way. When this "no man's

FIG. 90.—FOUNTAIN AT GOODRICH HOUSE.

FIG. 91.—GOODRICH HOUSE: FROM VIEW POINT "B" ON PLAN.

FIG. 92.—FROM VIEW POINT "A" ON PLAN (FIG. 89).

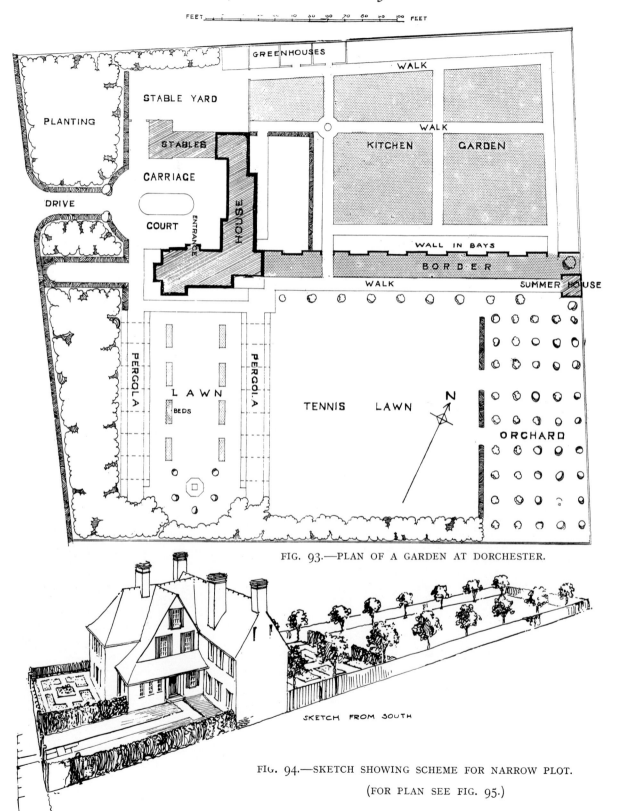

FIG. 93.—PLAN OF A GARDEN AT DORCHESTER.

SKETCH FROM SOUTH

FIG. 94.—SKETCH SHOWING SCHEME FOR NARROW PLOT.

(FOR PLAN SEE FIG. 95.)

land " has been passed we reach the garden proper, and notice on the left a pretty masonry fountain, illustrated in Fig. 90. The setting-out of the rest of the garden is sufficiently indicated by the general plan (Fig. 89).

A site almost square and flat without natural features offers a blank cheque in the matter of design. In Fig. 93 is illustrated such a garden laid out at Dorchester, Dorset, by Mr. Morley Horder, the architect of the house. It shows a useful division of the space into flower and kitchen gardens. As Horman wrote in his *Vulgaria*, " the knotte garden serveth for pleasure, the potte garden for profitte." Importance is given to the scheme by the wall in alternate bays, which divides the two main divisions and ties them both to the house. A photograph of a similar wall in another garden is reproduced in Chapter X. The two long pergolas which reach out from the house southwards serve a like purpose. A word must also be written about the very useful plan of a narrow suburban garden site shown in Fig. 95, and by sketch in Fig. 94. The ground treated measures only fifty by two hundred and ten feet. The garden on the entrance side is happily managed. It is divided by a tall yew hedge running east and west, so that a pretty little square garden, walled on the north and west sides, is provided for the sole pleasure of the servants. The entrance court adjoining it is left perfectly simple with grass margins to the paved walk. Flowers are concentrated on the low terrace, which is reached from the loggia. A hedge divides it from the tennis lawn, which is surrounded by lime trees, presently to be pleached. The success of the scheme is the result in no small measure of not attempting too much, which is the usual fault in very limited gardens.

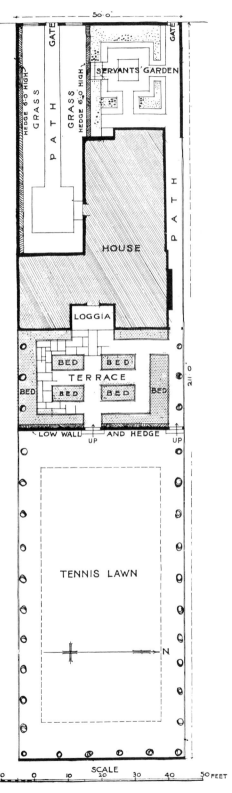

FIG. 95.—GOOD ARRANGEMENT OF NARROW PLOT.

CHAPTER VIII.—ON HILLSIDE GARDENS.

Lady Mary Wortley Montagu on Terraces—Stairways—Terraced Gardens—Inexpensive Materials—Various Examples.

NO site gives such great opportunity to the designer as one that slopes sharply. Whether from the point of view of house or garden, it is a moot point whether it is better that the slope shall be *downwards* from north to south, or with an upward slope southwards. Assuming that the house is to face south, the former disposition means an open and the latter an enclosed view. Most people prefer an open outlook, but there is a feeling of comfort about seeing one's own boundaries that needs to be taken into account. Generally, however, an alternative is not available, and our site has to be accepted as Nature fashioned it. When a hillside is considered purely from the point of view of garden design, it is obvious that its chief merit is that it calls for the free use of terracing and steps, and no other two features of garden architecture give so great an opportunity for varied and striking treatment. Bacon said that a bay window was the place for conference, and one may pay equal heed to a more lightsome author in her definition of a terrace. Writing from Hinchinbrook to her husband a few months after her marriage, Lady Mary Wortley Montagu tells him, "I walked yesterday two hours on the terrace," and again a few days later, "The terrace is my place consecrated to meditation, which I observe to be gay or grave, as the sun shows or hides his face." *Solvitur ambulando* is always a good rule, and a terrace walk, with its unchanging prospect and the sense of security given by its balustraded walls, is always friendly to quiet thought. It keeps the mind free from that hint of surprise which tickles the fancy of the true country lover in the turns even of the most quiet lane.

That the creation of artificial levels is not, however, the only way to deal with a hilly site is clear from the first illustration of this chapter. It shows the admirable effect of

FIG. 96.—TREATMENT OF SLOPING GROUND WITHOUT STAIRWAY.

FIG. 97.—AT HURTWOOD, SURREY : A STEEP ASCENT.

a broad sloping grass path between two yew hedges at Hurtwood, Surrey. It will be noted that the size of this part of the garden is considerable, and it is precisely this element which makes its success. A like treatment on a small scale would tend to dulness, and we may turn therefore to the stepped treatment of another part of the same garden. The ground covered by the stairway shown in Fig. 97 is quite small in extent, and therefore serves as a guide for the treatment of other steep sites. No little of its charm is in the contrast between the formal masonry of the steps and landings and the luxuriant growths which border them. In Fig. 99, which shows a design by Mr. C. E. Mallows, a similar treatment is indicated, but for a site with a far gentler slope. This enables very broad steps to be used without " risers," and does away with the need for landings, which are essential in the case of steeper stairways. It should be borne in mind that it is rather troublesome to walk up and down easy stairways with broad treads of this type unless each tread is broad enough to make it comfortable to take two steps to each. This suitable width is indicated in Mr. Mallows' drawing, but no definite dimensions are given here, as everyone can easily experiment for himself and fix on a width which he thinks most comfortable.

We may now consider the use that has been made of terracing by Mr. Thomas Young, who laid out the garden at Mr. G. Muntzer's house, Littleholme, Guildford, Surrey, in conjunction with Mr. Voysey, who was the architect for the house. The plan and section (Fig. 100) show clearly to what good account the hillside has been put. When the construction of the approach from the road was in hand, the hill showed the defects of its qualities, for the slope on the north side was very awkward. On the south side of the house a wide paved terrace has been provided with a pleasant double staircase leading down to a small grass garden surrounded by yew hedges, and provided with a pond and sundial. The little plateau so formed is held up on its south side by a curved brick bastion, which appears in Fig. 102.

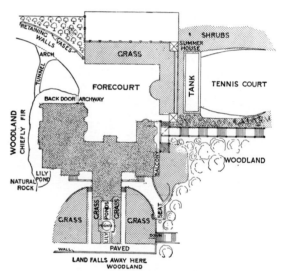

FIG. 98.—HURTWOOD : PLAN OF GARDENS NEAR HOUSE.

Westward of this, the garden is laid out in gradual terracing with flights of steps of easy gradient, which lead to what is now being planted as an orchard. The setting of the house on its precipitous site is perhaps best appreciated by the view shown in Fig. 101, which was taken from the loggia looking out across the terrace to the magnificent view that reaches to Bramley and Ewhurst. The garden walls are of purple brick coped with Bargate stone, and some of the terrace retaining walls are of flints which were dug from the site. On the front of the big lower bastion is an interesting gargoyle in wrought lead, which is illustrated in Chapter XIV. The making of such a garden naturally involved considerable excavation, and its owner has wisely proceeded with the work slowly. Our photographs hardly do the designer justice, because the garden as yet lacks the luxuriant growth which will soften the outlines of wall and terrace. It is useful to add that work of this kind, involving very considerable excavation, is a costly matter. The mere work of digging and wall-building, the construction, in fact, of the carcass of the garden, cost over five

FIG. 99.—DESIGN BY MR. C. E. MALLOWS FOR STAIRWAY ON GENTLE SLOPE.

hundred pounds, and this takes no account of planting, but the money has been worthily spent.

Sometimes, as at Hurtwood Edge (Fig. 105), the obviously right placing of the house with reference to aspect and view brings it about that the slope is at an angle with the chief front. It is a dangerous enterprise to plan a terraced garden on irregular lines in order to follow an erratic contour, and a geometrical, or at least symmetrical, shape will almost always be the best. The perspective view reproduced in Fig. 105 represents the original design of the garden (not yet carried out entirely). It shows how delightful a feature may be made of the tall buttress with its pier at one corner of the terrace. The natural fall of the site gave an architectural opportunity which Mr. Arthur T. Bolton, who designed the house,

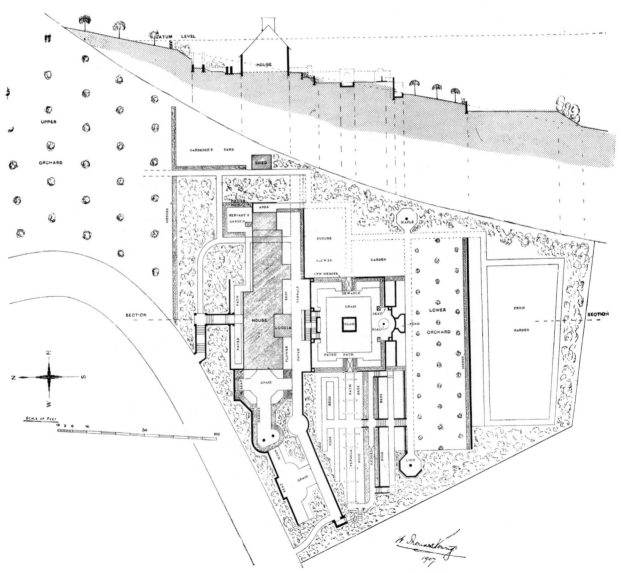

FIG 100.—LITTLEHOLME, GUILDFORD: PLAN AND SECTION SHOWING TREATMENT OF SLOPING SITE
BY MR. THOMAS YOUNG.

FIG. 101.—LITTLEHOLME, GUILDFORD: VIEW FROM LOGGIA ACROSS FIRST AND SECOND TERRACES.

FIG. 102.—LITTLEHOLME, GUILDFORD: TERRACES AND STAIRS FROM SOUTH-WEST.

was not slow to grasp. The plan, shown in Fig. 108, elucidates the scheme, and the neighbouring views mark the happy effect of the upper terrace of the house and the balustrading built up of curved tiles. The stair in the foreground of Fig. 106 is part of a simpler scheme of treatment than that originally planned. An unpretentious

FIG. 103.—LITTLEHOLME: SHOWING OUTLINE
OF UPPER TERRACE,—

FIG. 104.—AND THE TERRACE STAIRS.

FIG. 105—HURTWOOD EDGE : SCHEME FOR GARDEN.

FIG. 106 —HURTWOOD EDGE: TERRACE FROM BELOW.

FIG. 107.—THE TERRACE.

but satisfactory way of dealing with a sloping site in a small garden is shown in Fig. 109, which illustrates the garden at The Barn, Witley, Reading. Mr. Frank Chesterton has done no

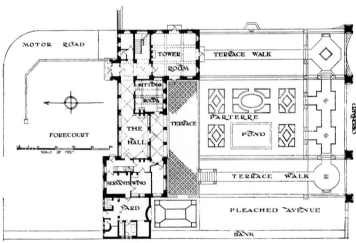

FIG. 108.—HURTWOOD EDGE: PLAN OF GARDEN SCHEME.

more than provide a short flight of steps, between dwarf walls, which leads to a little terrace. The materials deserve a word. In order to save cost the steps were built of rough purple

FIG. 109.—AT THE BARN, WITLEY, READING.

lumps of old burnt firebrick, which can sometimes be got from gasworks for a nominal sum, if not free. This must not be confounded with black gas clinker, which some misguided folk have used for rockeries. Clinker is as dismal and unpleasant a material as the old firebrick is attractive. The latter should not be used when the cost of good brick or tile or stone can be encompassed, but as a cheap alternative it is quite satisfactory. The view from the garden door at The Barn is a happy commentary on the pleasant air which a suburban garden can take on when some thought and very little money have gone to its making.

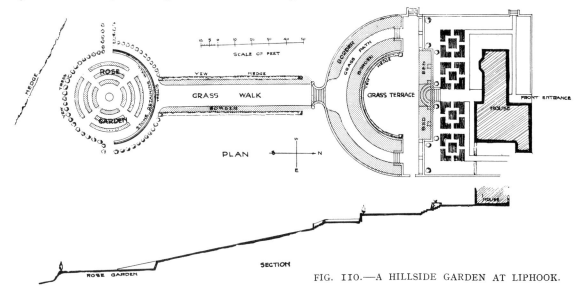

FIG. 110.—A HILLSIDE GARDEN AT LIPHOOK.

Another interesting treatment of a hillside site is shown in the photograph and plan (Figs. 110 and 111) of a garden at Liphook, designed by Mr. Inigo Triggs. In the front of the house is a terrace twenty-five feet wide, with steps leading down to a semi-circular grass terrace bordered by yew hedges. The next lower level is occupied by two flower borders divided by a grass path. From the end of the latter another flight of steps leads down to a green walk, which is enclosed on each side by yew hedges. This slopes down to a round rose garden. The section which is printed below the plan (Fig. 110) shows clearly how admirably the slope has been employed to give a succession of interesting garden incidents.

FIG. 111.—A HILLSIDE GARDEN AT LIPHOOK.

CHAPTER IX.—STEPS AND STAIRWAYS.

Approach Steps from Road—Stairways in Children's Dramas—Stepped Treatment for Gentle Slopes—Straight and Curved Stairs—Terrace Steps—Unformal Stairs.

THE notes on the treatment of hillside gardens given in the last chapter necessarily included some references to stairways associated directly with terracing, but the question of steps and their design arises in every kind of site, and in many parts of it. It is usual for a long stairway to be built of the same width throughout its flight, but a very pleasant variety can be got by widening it as it descends. The example shown in Fig. 112 is at Ardkinglas. It was devised in this manner by Sir Robert Lorimer, and very attractive it looks. Where the site of a house stands well above the roadway an interesting and dignified approach is secured by broad steps,

FIG. 112.—WIDENING STAIRWAY AT ARDKINGLAS.

FIG. 113.—CURVED ENTRANCE STAIRWAY AT OWLPEN MANOR.

FIG. 114.—AN UNRAILED STAIR.

FIG. 115.—AN ANGLED STAIRWAY WITH LOW COPING.

semi-circular on plan, such as is seen at Owlpen Manor (Fig. 113). When a considerable difference in level between two parts of a garden is masked by a wall pierced with a communicating door, an interesting feature can be made of the necessary steps. In gardens frequented by children—and it is a sad place that never knows their hurrying footsteps—unrailed stairs are not without danger. It is not difficult to see that, for young folk, the doorway illustrated in Fig. 114 demands to be made the scene for those swift comings and goings that belong to the search for treasure and the rescue of distressed maidens. The top step is obviously the place for the last stand of a devoted retainer, sworn to defend the brave lady of his absent lord. The shadow of the wall is no less clearly the place where conspirators will gather with hood and lantern, until the door flies open and the heroic knight leaps on them sword in hand. All this is right and proper, and it is one of the justifications of garden architecture that it provides a stage. But an un-guarded stair in conjunction with a doorway that conceals its dangers is a trap that may break young heads, and this aspect of the matter needs to be remembered. There is more of safety in the provision even of a low coping that follows the line of the steps, as in the angled stairway shown in Fig. 115. In the case of broad stepping that leads down to terrace walks it is often pleasant to break its line by a little pool or other projection from the upper level, such as is indicated by the treatment which Mr. Walter Cave employed at Ewelme Down (Fig. 116).

Small gardens of gentle slope must usually be formed as a series of shallow terraces for reasons of economy, and the stepped scheme at Home Place, Holt, designed by Professor E. S. Prior, will be a counsel of perfection to most people. Still, it is illustrated in

FIG. 116.—TERRACE STAIRWAY DIVIDED BY SMALL POOL.

FIG. 117.—TERRACE STAIRCASE OF FLAGS AND FLINT.

Figs. 117 and 118, because it is full of ideas that are capable of being interpreted on a smaller scale. The characteristic and beautiful house is built of flint and tile, and its south side is planned " sun-trap " fashion. A curved flight of steps leads down from the main terrace to a long stairway of gentle descent with wide, shallow treads. This

FIG. 118.—AT HOME PLACE, NORFOLK.

is divided down the middle by a long stepped pool, which is richly hospitable to free-growing water plants (Fig. 117).

Returning, however, to strictly small gardens, it may be said that many of them lose in attractiveness by the careless treatment of the short stairways which lead from one level to another. It is not always realised how much additional charm is given by the well-conceived design of such details, or how great a variety lies open to the straying choice. Steps need to be considered in relation to the retaining walls, in which

FIG. 119.—ALTERNATION OF ROUND AND SQUARE STEPS.

they often make a break. They should have wide treads and low " risers " so that they are easy-going. Too great a regularity in their building is generally to be avoided. Rough rubble masonry is to be preferred to ashlar, where stone and not brick is the material, but the rustic character should not be overdone. Great variety is to be attained by a happy conjunction of straight with curved steps, as is seen in Fig. 119, which shows also the value of rough

FIG. 120.—STEPPED APPROACH TO PERGOLA.

piers to mark the break in the retaining wall. This example is chosen from Island, Steep, designed by Messrs. Unsworth and Triggs. A similar treatment is illustrated in Fig. 120, which shows the entrance to a walled garden at Ewelme Down. A terrace stair at the same house, half-round on plan, is also shown in Fig. 122. The plea for the wide treads that make an easy-going stairway only holds good when practical considerations of site and convenience make it possible. Where there is a great break in levels a steep flight may be inevitable, and Fig. 123 shows how very pleasant it may look. It is rare that an approach road is very greatly higher in level than the ground floor level of the house, but this

FIG. 121.—DETACHED PORCH AND STAIR.

sometimes happens on a steep hillside. At Sulling-stead, near Hascombe, Mr. Lutyens has contrived an interesting way out of the difficulty. At the upper road level has been built a detached porch with a tiled roof carried on pillars. From this a brick stair winds down to a narrow forecourt, which divides the entrance door from the foot of the porch stairway by no more than a few feet.

In the contriving of the stairs from house terrace to lawn it is desirable to avoid the common mistake of making them too narrow.

FIG. 122 —ROUND STAIR ON TERRACE.

FIG. 123.—STEEP FLIGHT OF STEPS AT MATHERN.

Several examples are given which show stairs adequately designed in this respect. That illustrated in Fig. 124 is in the garden of a house in North - East Lancashire, designed by that able artist and attractive personality, the late Dan Gibson, who did so much to revive the type of architecture proper to the Lake District. The rough stone steps accord well with the dry-walling. Attention may also be drawn

FIG. 124.—ROUGHLY BUILT STAIR FROM TERRACE TO LAWN.

to the pool set in an embrasure of the wall. Another example is in a more regular and finished manner (Fig. 125). It is at a house designed by Mr. Lutyens, and the variety in the steps descending two ways is in charming contrast to the massive bulk of the retaining walls of the terrace. Very often it produces an excellent

FIG. 125.—TERRACE STEPS BY MR. LUTYENS.

FIG. 126.—BROAD STAIRWAY FROM TERRACE TO LAWN.

effect to provide a very broad flight of steps from the middle of the terrace to the lawn below, such as is suggested by the drawing by Mr. C. E. Mallows (Fig. 126).

In the chapter on " Water in the Formal Garden " many of the diverse schemes shown by photograph or drawing depend for their success on the steps with which the pools compose. The design by Mr. Inigo Triggs, now illustrated in Figs. 127 and 128, gives a hint for the treatment of a double stairway connecting two levels, and has a shaped pool for its central feature. This scheme could be applied very appropriately

FIG. 127.—DOUBLE STAIRWAY WITH POOL.

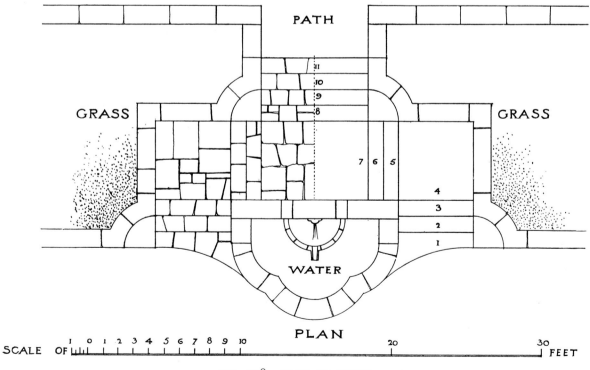

FIG. 128.—PLAN OF ABOVE.

FIG. 129.—SIMPLE STAIRWAY FOR A WOODLAND WALK.

to the descent from house terrace to sunk garden, or as the ascent from such sunk garden to a lawn beyond.

Although stairways are among the most useful elements in garden design, and give just opportunity for conscious architectural treatment, it is not always desirable to force the note of formality. In situations where Nature has been lavish with her wild charms the signs of the hand of man should be suppressed, so that nothing may appear to compete with effects of a kind that no designer can bring. Even in small gardens that are made on woodland sites there is often a green alley over-arched with trees which fleck the path with sunlit tracery. Of such a kind is the example illustrated in Fig. 129 The stone steps there are of the simplest, and show themselves to be perfectly right for their situation. The adding of flanking piers crowned by vase or statue would strike a note of artifice which would accord ill with the natural beauty of the scene.

CHAPTER X.—BALUSTRADES AND WALLS.

The Design of Balusters—The Imitation of Historical Examples—Walls and Parapets of Open Brickwork—Walls Surmounted by Beams—A Coronal Garden—Serpentine Walls—Building in Concrete.

TERRACE balustrading in stone of the sort shown in the picture below is a costly feature of garden architecture, and belongs rather to large schemes than to those which develop round a small house. Beyond illustrating as models this Jacobean example, and a modern application of the same treatment by Mr. Inigo Thomas at Rotherfield, in Figs. 132 and 133, it will, therefore, be enough to put in a claim for refinement in baluster design. In the terraces of great houses where

FIG. 130.—A JACOBEAN BALUSTRADE.

FIG. 131.—AT NEWTON FERRERS, CORNWALL.

the scale is big throughout, a certain heaviness of treatment is not only allowable but even necessary, but small schemes demand delicate handling. It is unsafe to rely upon historical examples for imitation merely because they look admirable in their own setting. We have to reckon with the glamour which age brings with weathering and lichen, and to beware. There are many features of old work which will not bear reproduction without looking garish to the point of vulgarity. It is difficult, moreover in the case of an old house or church, to draw a line between the emotional appeal of history and the strictly architectural merits, the more so as Time's way with buildings, as with men, is to soften them. The student of such things may amuse himself by wondering what would be the verdict of the sightseer concerning Roslyn Chapel if he were to see it in all its luxuriance, but fresh from

FIG. 132.—TERRACE BALUSTRADE AT ROTHERFIELD.

FIG. 133.—ROTHERFIELD : DETAILS OF TERRACE WALLS.

FIG. 134.—IN MOULDED BRICK.

the chisel, and without the mist of sentiment which rises from the legend of the Prentice Pillar. In considering the value of old work as a model for imitation it is necessary to study the material to which has been given various forms. The balusters at Newton Ferrers (Fig. 131) have a coarseness of outline which amounts almost to brutality, and makes them very unsuitable as models. Yet in their own place, and against the austere background

FIG. 135.—OPEN PARAPET OF CURVED TILES.

of an eighteenth century house, they are seen to be altogether admirable, because they are of Cornish granite. The form was determined by the intractable material and exactly suits it. From these notes it will be clear that it is impossible to lay down any rules for the design of terrace balustrades of stone; they form an integral part of the house, and are governed by the factors which determine its architectural treatment.

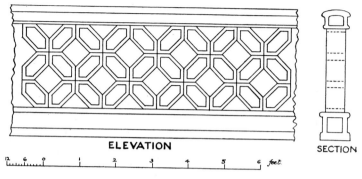

ELEVATION   SECTION

FIG. 136.—OF HOLLOW HEXAGONAL TILES.

Terrace walls of open brickwork make a simpler problem. Much can be done with tiles and bricks of ordinary forms in achieving interesting varieties of treatment. The wall illustrated in Fig. 134 shows bricks moulded after a Portuguese pattern, which give a light and lace-like effect. The short stretch of parapet which appears in Fig. 135 is of very pleasant appearance, but it is built up of ordinary elements. The rusticated piers are of thin red bricks, and the openwork of curved tiles, each made to a quarter of a circle. Fig. 136 shows a North Italian example of hollow hexagonal tiles with top rail and plinth. The expense of preparing moulds for a special size or shape of hand-made brick is trivial when it is spread over the making of a few thousands. Fig. 137 shows a design by Mr. Inigo Triggs for an attractive and unusual wall with tile capping and recurring panels filled with pierced and shaped bricks.

The walls of fruit gardens are best built in a straightforward way, but fancy may be let loose in designing the walls of a flower garden, especially if the treatment

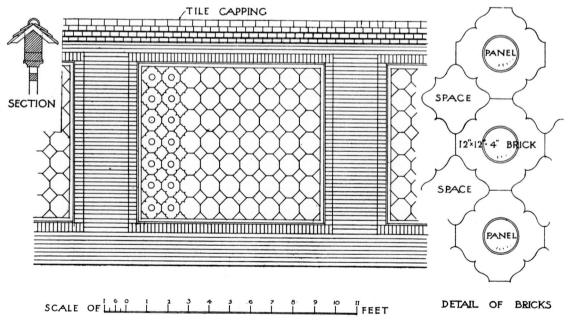

TILE CAPPING

SECTION

PANEL

SPACE

12"×12"×4" BRICK

SPACE

PANEL

SCALE OF ⌐⌐⌐⌐ FEET

DETAIL OF BRICKS

FIG. 137.—WALL WITH OPENWORK PANELS.

contemplated lends changefulness to variety of growth. Very often the designer of a small garden is faced by the difficulty of giving it privacy, and shrinks from the uninteresting solution of building a plain high wall. In such a case the two schemes indicated in Figs. 138 and 139 suggest happy alternatives, the former of which appears in a modified form in the picture (Fig. 68) of Mr. Inigo Triggs' own garden at Liphook. It shows a stone wall eighteen inches thick, and it is desirable, where choice is possible, to build it of sandstone in order that it may weather to a pleasant colour. This type of garden masonry looks best when the joints are well raked out, so that each individual stone may show distinctly. The piers are spaced ten feet apart, and are connected by curves. Rough beams about four inches square, with cross-pieces about two inches square, are supported on the piers, and roses and other creeping plants are trained to intertwine amid the woodwork. In Fig. 139 a similar arrangement is shown for brick

FIG. 138.—STONE WALL WITH TIMBERED PIERS.   FIG. 139.—THE SAME IN BRICK WITH FLOWER BOXES.

walls, with this interesting difference : the piers for a distance of two feet from the top and the boxes at their sides are of four and a-half inch brickwork filled with earth. In the illustration these receptacles are shown in broken section rather than with appropriate plants growing, in order that the method of construction may be clear. Each should be drained with a small pipe about one inch in diameter, which will throw the drainage-water clear of the wall on its far side. The spacing of the piers in this case, as in the last, should be about ten feet, and a good height for either type is eight feet, the walls thus being about five feet. Where bricks are used, red is the best colour. If only inferior bricks are available, the walls should be rough-cast or cemented (a finishing coat being laid very roughly), and should show the marks of the wooden float. Much more ambitious and very successful is the design of the wall that encircles a little round garden (called the Coronal) at Athelhampton, designed by Mr. Inigo Thomas. Its parapet dips in a series of half rounds, and the rising

FIG. 140.—THE CORONAL: ROUND-WALLED GARDEN AT ATHELHAMPTON.

FIG. 141.—SERPENTINE WALL AT HEVENINGHAM HALL.

parts between are crowned with stone obelisks, round which climbing roses have wound their tender way. It is an admirable device for the treatment of a small space, and could be carried out in a simpler fashion in brick without undue expenditure (Fig. 140).

Among the less usual forms of brick walls a high place must be given to those on a serpentine plan, and for several reasons. If built only about five feet high, they can be constructed a single brick thick. This is not safe with a straight wall of the same height, which should be two bricks thick. The extra length of single brickwork occasioned by the wavy plan only means an addition of about one-quarter to the cubic measurement. This means that a ribbon wall stretching a hundred feet would involve only five-eighths to three-quarters the cost of a straight wall covering the same distance. There are, moreover, cultural advantages. The concave faces on the south side of a serpentine wall serve in some sort as sun-traps, and are therefore kindly to wall fruit. The example at Heveningham Hall (Fig. 141) is nearly ten feet high, and is therefore more than a single brick thick, but even tall walls can be built more cheaply serpentine fashion than straight. In laying out a flower border under such a wall it would be well to emphasise the unusual line by waving the outline of the border. The obvious method is a simple reversal of the wavy line,

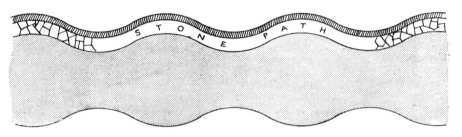

FIG. 142.—FLOWER–BED AGAINST SERPENTINE WALL—

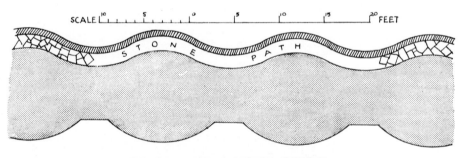

FIG. 143.—AND A BETTER OUTLINE.

as shown in Fig. 142, but that gives a rather weak effect, and it is better to rely on a more geometrical setting-out, as indicated in Fig. 143. As such a flower border would work out very wide at the points where the convex curve is opposed to the concave recessing of the wall, the wise method with all wide borders under walls—viz., of providing a narrow path between wall and bed—is all the more valuable. This treatment is indicated in both plans. Eighteen inches is a sufficient width for such a path.

It is difficult to establish the date when serpentine walls first came into vogue, but it is unlikely that it was before the middle of the eighteenth century. Miss Phillimore, in her *Life of Wren*, when writing of Wraxall Abbey, Warwickshire, which was bought by the great architect in his old age, says, "Sir Christopher is said to have designed the kitchen garden wall, which is built in semi-circles." This wall is not strictly serpentine, but set out in half-circles with straight stretches connecting them : the idea is, however, the same. A device of this kind is just one of the things with which the inventiveness of Wren is likely to have played. As, however,

FIG. 144.—WALL WITH SQUARE BREAKS.

FIG. 145.—CONCRETE WALLS AT LAMBAY.

FIG. 146.—WALL MASKING KITCHEN QUARTERS.

1789 is on a stone of the wall, his authorship must be doubted. The writer of this has seen a serpentine wall at a Suffolk house of late in the eighteenth century. A good modern example, a single brick thick, designed by Mr. F. W. Troup, is illustrated in *Small Country Houses of To-day.* Built with the same purpose as a serpentine wall, *i.e.*, to give somewhat sheltered bays for fruit, is the straight wall with square breaks at a Buckinghamshire house designed by Mr. P. Morley Horder. It is the better, both practically and in appearance, for its tiled ridge. In districts where both stone and brick are more costly than concrete, the latter material is useful for garden walls. In Fig. 145 is illustrated a concrete wall of very good appearance, designed by Mr. Lutyens for the gardens of Lambay Castle. The terminal posts are given almost a Doric character by the marks left by the wood boxing set up temporarily, into which the half-liquid concrete was poured. An admirable crown is given to the wall by dark grey Dutch pantiles. The building of garden walls to mask kitchen courts and other spaces, which are necessarily untidy at times, belongs rather to the design of the house than of the garden, but one example is illustrated in Fig. 146 because of its intrinsically garden treatment. A stout trellis is set penthouse-fashion from the ridged screen wall (in the foreground of the picture) to the wall of the house, and offers hospitality to such creepers as are light enough not to interfere too much with the usefulness of the windows beneath.

CHAPTER XI.—CLIMBING AND OTHER PLANTS ON WALLS AND HOUSES.

Misuse of Ivy—Of Ampelopsis—Of Wistaria—Various Climbers—Shrubs Trained to Walls.

THE appearance of many a house is made or marred by the wise or injudicious use of climbing plants. A house of no special character may become a thing of beauty ; one of architectural value may have that whole value obliterated and the structure greatly damaged. In the latter case the danger is so great and negligence so frequent that it will be well to offer some words of warning. Many a

fine old gateway of carefully-designed brickwork or of wrought stone has been allowed to become smothered with ivy. Ivy is of the nature of a true hard-wooded tree. When the mortar has fallen out of the joints of old masonry, these open joints are just the places seized upon by the fast-growing ivy shoots. The shoot, at first a bare eighth of an inch thick, quickly swells, hardening as it grows. Soon it fills the joint, and, ever increasing, acts as a wedge with irresistible power, and eventually forces the stones apart. Ancient buildings and ruins that are of historical and archæological interest are the easiest and most usual prey of the devastating ivy, but many fine old houses throughout the land are even now suffering from its dangerous overgrowth. In some cases, from the pictorial point of view, the need for abolishing the ivy is something of a misfortune, especially in the case of old ruins ; but its removal is a necessity if the evil is not to be aggravated. In the case of a new bare wall where the joints are sound, and level with the face of the

FIG. 147.—OVERGROWTH OF IVY ON SCULPTURED GATEWAY.

FIG. 148.—OVERGROWTH OF IVY ON GATE-PIER AND GARDEN-HOUSE.

FIG. 149.—OVERGROWTH OF IVY ON GATE-PIER AND WALL.

FIG. 150.—STONE GATEWAY MODERATELY CLOTHED.

brickwork, there is no danger, and the ivy is even protective, the leaves throwing off the wet. But the plant is quick to detect and occupy any opening, when danger and damage may quickly follow.

The fine and boldly-treated brick piers to wrought-iron gates shewn in Figs. 148 and 149 have been smothered with ivy, and not the piers only, but also the rather important point where the pier rises from the wall. This is specially deplorable in the picture from the outside of one of the entrances to the walled garden, with the flight of uncommon circular brick steps (Fig. 149). It may be noted incidentally that this illustration shows another defect very common in gardens where there is no critical eye ever on the watch for such blemishes. The level of the path has shrunk away several inches, leaving the under-course of brickwork exposed, and making the whole step inconveniently high as well as entirely out of proportion. In the case of the inner view, where one of the brick piers is, happily, free, the summer-house with arched doorway is also over-smothered with ivy (Fig. 148). We believe that the overgrowth of ivy on this fine example of gateway treatment has been removed, but are glad that the piers were photographed in their overdone state as a useful warning. The beautiful eighteenth century gateway shewn in Fig. 147, photographed in 1903, but now, we hope, cleared, shows ivy obliterating the architrave and entablature of an ornate design. There is no harm in the slight encroachment of a leaf or two of the flanking magnolias; nobility of form in foliage is a desirable accompaniment to good architecture, but it should only be allowed to accompany, not to oppress—still less to overwhelm.

FIG. 151.—WISTARIA MISPLACED.

It is not the fault of the ivy, a precious and beautiful climbing plant—it is the misuse of ivy and the neglect of due control that we desire to emphasise. Ivy was largely used in decorative schemes by the French in the eighteenth century and later, and to this day is cleverly employed as screening walls of greenery on railings and treillage. It deserves to be much more used as a screen plant, and if a large unbroken surface should appear monotonous, the want of variety can be remedied by training over it a tracery of some other climber, such as Clematis Flammula or Virginia creeper. Another stone gateway (Fig. 150) is reasonably clothed with rose and vine foliage; but their growth is already quite enough—a little more and it would be overdone. The popular and, in its place, valuable Ampelopsis Veitchii has much to answer for. It has perceptibly harmed the fine brickwork of some of the old Tudor buildings at Hampton Court—not only smothering the architecture but actually damaging the surface. The plant clings by little roundish suckers; in time these become dry and as hard as wire. When the harmful growth was at last recognised on some of the portions of the palace built by Cardinal Wolsey, and it was cleared away, the dry suckers held so tightly that they could not be dislodged without bringing away some of the face of the brick.

In the case of the wistaria forming an outer curtain to a pointed-arched window one may easily guess how such an odd misuse of a fine plant may have occurred

FIG. 152.—RAMBLING ROSES, VINE AND IVY ON ROUGH BUILDINGS.

(Fig. 151). It is evident that it was forbidden to drive supporting nails or staples into the joints of the stonework, and that the only apparent alternative was to fasten the plant to the iron bars of the window itself. The still simpler alternative was overlooked, namely, that of refraining from the use of a plant requiring nailing on a wall where it could not be nailed. The same picture shows an error only too common in gardens—that of having a bed of small plants in immediate connection with important masonry. The wistaria, with its probable ultimate fate, is the more to be regretted because the plant itself is in fine, young vigour, having got over the earlier stage of standing still for the first few years, as is the way of its kind. This fine plant may

be used in many ways — on garden and house walls, on pergolas and arbours. The newer Japanese kind (*W. multijuga*) is as easily grown as the older *W. Chinensis*, but although the racemes of flower are much longer, it is hardly a more attractive plant than the better-known kind.

Besides the walls where climbing plants are grown for their own beauty there are places in nearly every garden where it is desirable to clothe some rough building or to cover or screen something un-sightly (Fig. 152). For this the rougher of the rambling roses and the wilder of the clematises are in-valuable. The native *C. Vitalba* covers very large spaces, and grows fast. Clematis montana is eager

FIG. 153.—CLEMATIS MONTANA.

to rush up to a considerable height and then to tumble over with sheets of graceful foliage and cataracts of pure white bloom (Fig. 153). *Clematis Flammula* rambles widely among other growths, flowering in September ; it is followed closely by *C. paniculata* in October. Space only allows of the barest mention of other good climbing plants—*clematis* species such as the yellow-bloomed *C. graveolens ;* in choicest gardening the splendid varieties of the Japanese *C. patens* and the Chinese *C. lanuginosa*, and the many pretty hybrids of *C. viticella.* Then we have *Bignonia radicans* with its ash-like leaves and trumpet flowers of orange and scarlet ; *Solanum crispum* and *S. jasminoides.* Grape vines of the Chasselas class form perhaps the most beautiful of all wall covering, especially for sheltered, quiet places where bright flowers are not absolutely needed ; but among vines, where colour is wanted, there is the crimson-foliaged claret vine and *Vitis Coignetiæ,* brilliant-hued in autumn. Roses one can but barely touch upon except to say that warm walls are only suitable for teas and noisettes.

Then there are the numbers of shrubs, which, though not of a climbing habit, are thoroughly satisfactory when trained to walls. Figs for important foliage ; *Pyrus japonica* and the winter-sweet (*Chimonanthus*) for winter bloom ; *Abutilon vitifolium,* of extreme beauty and strangely little planted ; ceanothus of several kinds ; *Buddleia variabilis Veitchii,* choisya, the brittle *Robinia hispida,* with flower-clusters something like wistaria, but of a charming pink colour. Then for cold exposures the common guelder rose makes a capital wall plant, and is well accompanied by Clematis montana running through it, flowering at the same time, and adding to the pretty picture of copious white bloom. Another happy mixture for a cool wall is the handsome shrubby spiræa, *S. lindleyana,* with its cream-coloured bloom and fine pinnate leaves. *Clematis Flammula* trained through this forms another desirable combination. Laurustinus, not only the common but also the black, and the later-blooming *L. lucidus* are all excellent for training to cool walls.

Fig. 154.—Ampelopsis Veitchii restricted in growth
so that the whole wall face is not covered.

CHAPTER XII.—RETAINING WALLS AND THEIR PLANTING.

Hillside Sites—Turf Banks—Dry Walling—Grouping in Planted Dry Walls in Sun and Shade—Construction—Importance of Ramming—Steps.

MANY gardens that are on hillsides are of necessity arranged in a succession of terraces needing retaining walls to support each succeeding level. In the case of gardens made fifty years ago, before better influences prevailed, the difficulty was got over by making turf banks. But it is very rarely that a turf bank is a desirable feature in a garden; more often it is distinctly ugly, or, at the best, quite uninteresting, while it is always difficult to mow and burns badly if on a southern slope. Where such a turf bank remains, it would, in nearly every case, be better to convert it into a wall; the line of the wall being taken at halfway down the slope and carried to the lower level, the earth excavated at the bottom filling up above. When this is done space is gained both above and below, while the wall itself becomes precious gardening ground; for if built as a " dry wall," that is to say, with earth joints instead of mortar, the joints, and the chinks in the case of uneven stones, are the happiest possible places for the growing of nearly all alpines, or if the wall

FIG. 155.—THIN SLATE STONES LAID LEVEL.

FIG. 156—BRICK DRY WALLING, PLANTED WITH PANSIES, SNAPDRAGONS, LONDON PRIDE AND OTHER SAXIFRAGES, WITH TUFTED PANSIES AT THE FOOT.

is of some size and height, for a number of our best garden plants.   Then the fact of the plants being raised some feet above the ground brings them into the most convenient range of sight.   Some lovely little alpines at easy eye-level can be much more comfortably and leisurely examined than in the ordinary rock garden ; all their little beauties of form, colour and scent can be enjoyed and appreciated to the full. Many of them grow naturally in rocky clefts, hanging down in sheets of loveliness, so that the wall shows, in a better way than any other kind of gardening, the real habit and character of the plant—its own method of growing, enjoying life and displaying beauty.

In the case of such planted walls it is best to have no flower-border at the foot, but to have a border above, occupying, in the case of a converted grass bank, what would represent the upper half of the bank.   It is well to fill it with a good proportion of things of bushy habit, such as bush roses, Scotch briars, lavender, rosemary, olearias, phlomis and so on.   In this way the border forms a protecting parapet, while the whole wall-face is free for use.   It also allows of combining the upper planting with that of the wall in a way that always proves satisfactory ; some of the plants of the top being also placed in the upper joints.   But in a garden where there are many planted walls monotony of treatment is avoided by having in some part rambling roses at the top to tumble over, with a thinner growth of tea roses at the foot, and but little planted in the wall-joints.

As in arranging flower-borders, it is well to place the plants in groups of a fair quantity of one thing at a time ;   and, in the case of small plants, such as thrift or London Pride, to put them fairly close together.   If they are spaced apart at even distances they look like buttons ;   but even when this has been done, either inadvertently or by an unpractised hand, it is easily remedied by adding a few plants to make the group hang together.   Though it is advised that there should be no border at the foot of a planted dry wall, yet it looks well to have its junction with the grass or gravel broken here and there by some plant that enjoys such a place, as, for example, *Iris stylosa* or *Plumbago larpentæ* in a sunny aspect, or hardy ferns and Welsh poppy and small pansies in a shady one.   It is well also to make careful combinations of colour, for they not only give the prettiest pictures, but also that restful feeling of some one idea completely presented that is so desirable, so easy to accomplish, and yet so rarely seen in gardens.   As an example, on a sunny wall there may be a colour-scheme of grey with purple of various shades, white and pale pink, composed of dwarf lavender, nepeta, aubrietia, cerastium, Helianthemums of the kinds that have grey leaves and white and pale pink bloom, rock pinks, stachys, the dwarf artemisias and Achillea umbellata, and in the border above, yuccas, lavender, rosemary, the larger euphorbias, China roses, phlomis and santolina with white and pink snapdragons.   Phlomis and santolina both have yellow flowers, but a slight break of yellow would harm the effect but little during their time of bloom, while both are of year-long value for their good grey foliage ; moreover, it is easy to remove the santolina bloom, which comes on shoots that are quite separate from the foliage. If it were quite a high wall, larger plants could be used, especially in the upper half. Yuccas are grand coming out of rocky chinks high up, and gypsophila in great clouds, and centranthus (the red valerian) in big bushy masses.

On a shady wall there would be a preponderance of good greenery of hardy ferns, male fern and hart's-tongue, with the smaller ferns, woodsia, cheilanthes, adiantum and allosorus, with Welsh poppies, corydalis, mimulus and the smaller alpine bell-flowers, such as the lovely little Campanula pusilla, both blue and white, and the rather larger carpatica and eriocarpa.   Then if the shady wall was of good size there would be columbines in quantity, white foxgloves and mulleins growing with splendid vigour and enjoying the cool root-run among the stones.

The way the walls are put up is of the utmost importance, for on the way it is done depends not only the appearance but the stability. Dry walling made rightly may be carried up twelve feet or more, even in recently disturbed soil, while if wrongly or negligently done a wall only three feet high will come down with the first heavy storm of rain. The following description will help those who wish to build their own walls, and to an intelligent amateur there is hardly a department of garden work that is more interesting and even delightful, especially where there is good local stone. Where there is no stone a dry wall can be built of brick, but this is duller work and is best done by a trained bricklayer. In some cases, in brick retaining walls a brick or half-brick is left out to give more space for inserting plants, or the whole is built in mortar, leaving such spaces only for planting ; but the earth joint throughout is rather more satisfactory, giving more freedom for the shaping of the groups.

The wall should lie back a little—" batter back " is the technical word, derived, no doubt, as are so many of our words for tools and building, from the French. It

FIG. 157.—A TEN-FOOT WALL PLANTED WITH GYPSOPHILA, VALERIAN, SANTOLINA, ROCK PINKS AND CERASTIUM, LUPINES AND ROSEMARY AT TOP.

suggests a near relationship to *abattre*, to beat down or beat back. As a good general rule it may batter back in the proportion of one foot in six of height. Every stone, lying on its natural bed at right angles to the sloped-back face, has the back a little lower than the front. It follows that every drop of rain that falls on the face of the wall runs into the next joint, to the benefit of the plants. If a dry wall is built on solid ground it needs but little foundation. Two thin courses under ground will be enough. The tilting back of the stones is begun under ground, then the upper courses follow naturally. A bed of earth is laid between each course and the ends of the stones, as if it was mortar. As the work comes out of the ground, and, indeed, from the very beginning, the loose soil is rammed in behind and between all the stones that project backward. It is upon firm and quite conscientious ramming that the stability of the wall depends. Labourers are apt to scamp it ; even experienced builders and foremen, unless they have had special experience in dry walling, do not give it the unremitting attention that it requires. This tight ramming cannot be too strongly insisted on or the absolute need of it too often repeated. Ram as tightly

FIG. 158.—BRICK DRY WALLING PLANTED WITH RAMBLING ROSES ABOVE AND TEA ROSES BELOW.

FIG. 159.—COLOUR SCHEME IN DRY WALL OF PURPLISH-GREY BRICK. CERASTIUM, WHITE AND
LILAC TUFTED PANSY AT FOOT; CHINA ROSES ABOVE.

FIG. 160.—PALE PINK ROSE, VALERIAN, CERASTIUM AND ROCK PINK IN A ROUGH STONE WALL.

as possible and on every part of the back of the walling. If the whole thing is in "made ground" it must all be rammed, but the part just behind the stones is the vulnerable point. If the ramming is neglected or is insufficient the wall will either come down in heavy rain or will bulge at various points in a manner that is very unsightly.

It is always best to lay the stones level as to right and left and on their natural bed, that is, the same way up as they lay in the quarry; they both look better and stand better. They can be either sorted into those of approximately the same thickness for separate courses, or the thinner stones laid to come level with the thicker. All "random" walling is ugly and unrestful, giving the impression of a wilful violation of simple laws of structure. When there are pieces of small broken stone to be disposed of, they can be rammed in with the earth at the back of the wall, making quite sure that no cavities are left. The roots of the wall plants

FIG. 161.—WHITE FOXGLOVE IN DRY WALLING OF LARGE STONES.

like nothing better than to cling to the cool and always moist stone surfaces.

A dry wall cannot be built against a scarp of hard sand or chalk. Enough must be taken out at the back to allow for fresh filling and ramming. Builders often think they can build against a solid scarp, but the experiment always results in disaster.

FIG. 162.—BRICK WALL WITH SPACES LEFT FOR PLANTS.

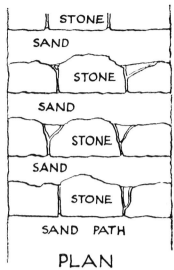
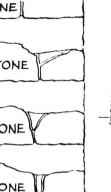

PLAN

FIG. 163.—STEPS WITH FRONT
EDGES ONLY OF STONE.

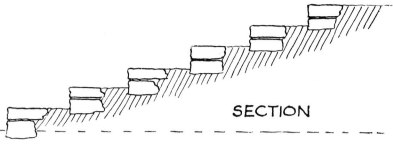

FIG. 165.—STEPS WITH FRONT EDGES ONLY OF STONE.

If the scarp is of actual rock there is no need for the wall except in cases where the strata tip down forward, when plants could not be comfortably grown. But in such a case it would be better to have some of the wilder clematis or roses planted at the top to wreathe and trail over the rocky surface.

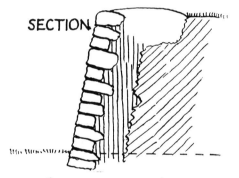

FIG. 164.—DRY WALLING (SECTION). TIGHTLY RAMMED EARTH SHOWN BY VERTICAL HATCHING.

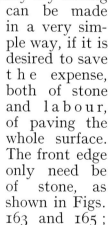

The steps that accompany dry walling can be made in a very simple way, if it is desired to save the expense, both of stone and labour, of paving the whole surface. The front edge only need be of stone, as shown in Figs. 163 and 165;

FIG. 166.—DRY WALL (SECTION) SHOWING PLANTING OF TOP AND FACE.

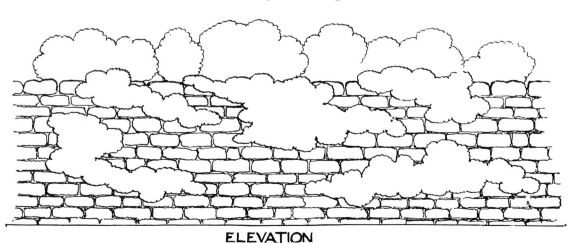

ELEVATION

FIG. 167.—ELEVATION OF PLANTED WALL, SHOWING GROUPING.

the stones chosen or trimmed so that they have fairly good front edges and so that they come together at the joints for at least a part of their depth. To give better cohesion at the back a triangular piece can easily be fitted, as shown in Fig. 163. The joints are then cemented, the cement joint being kept down low and as much out of sight as possible. Then the whole thing will hold together and little mosses will grow in the upper parts of the joints. On the sides and even towards the earthy back of the step tiny things like the smaller stonecrops and the smallest bell-flowers can be grown. Other near plants will also seed over the space, and in a few years the problem will be how to repress rather than encourage the quantity of plants that are only too willing to invade the steps. The wider and shallower the steps the pleasanter they are to go up and down—the extreme of comfort being a step from four to five inches high and twenty-two to twenty-four inches from front to back ; such steps as one may run up and down.

The planting of the joints of pavements gives scope for much judicious work, but needs great care and restraint. There should be no inconvenient invasion of plants. The idea of such planting has so greatly attracted garden enthusiasts that in many cases it has been carried too far. It should be remembered that the first purpose of a paved space is to provide a dry, level place for easy progression. If nearly every joint is filled with plants, those who pass along will either be obliged to keep their eyes on the ground or they will frequently feel, with a pang of regret, that some pretty thing has either been trodden under foot or inadvertently kicked against and dislodged. It is better to keep all the middle space free, or to attempt to do so, for small plants like these joints so well that they are apt both to run and seed freely within their welcome shelter.

CHAPTER XIII.—YEW AND OTHER HEDGES.

Yew Hedges in Ancient Gardens—In Modern Use—Other Trees for Hedges—Box—
Holly—Privet—Laurel—Beech—Hornbeam—Thorough Planting—Topiary Work.

WHEN the great English houses were built that no longer needed to be fortresses ;
when their windows might safely look abroad into the open country instead
of giving on to an inner court ; then also the pleasure garden, which had
hitherto been necessarily restricted, was greatly enlarged and its many possibilities
were developed. Whether it was that the tradition of the old need of walled protection was still in every man's mind, or whether the wonderful sense of fitness that
characterised the work of our Tudor and Jacobean ancestors was the impelling agency
we know not, but it is clear that they at once adopted the system of surrounding and
subdividing their gardens with hedges of living greenery. They rightly chose the

FIG. 168.—LAWN ENCLOSED BY ANCIENT TRIMMED YEWS.

FIG. 169.—CLEEVE PRIOR: THE TWELVE APOSTLES.

English yew as the tree that should conform to their will as green walls and ornaments in their gardens of formal design. Some actual examples remain, while traces of the use of green yew, clipped and regulated, as important portions of the garden plan, are so frequent as to point to its general use. In some cases of remaining examples the original design is distorted or entirely lost, and yet a mysterious and strangely attractive charm remains ; while in others some kind of symmetry has been maintained (Fig. 168). There are examples of noble use from old times in gardens of quite moderate size. The ancient yews at Cleeve Prior (Fig. 169), known as the Twelve Apostles, stand in six stately pairs flanking the paved walk to a modest manor house. At a little more than halfway of their height each pair stretches out branches to the next, forming a connecting arch, so that a framed garden scene, five times repeated, is visible from right and left. Hedges of yew with turf alone have an

FIG. 170.—AN ANCIENT BOWLING GREEN.

extraordinary quality of repose—of inspiring a sentiment of refreshing contentment. One thinks, with abounding satisfaction of many an ancient bowling green, with its bright, short turf underfoot, its deep green sides of yew, or yew and quiet wall, and nothing more but the sky above and perhaps some masses of encompassing trees (Figs. 170 and 171). Compared with the yew no tree is so patient of coercion, so protective in its close growth, or so effective as a background to the bright bloom of parterre or flower-border (Fig. 172). Its docility to shaping into wall, niche, arch and column is so complete and convenient that it comes first among growing things as a means of expression in that domain of design that lies between architecture and gardening. Our architects and garden designers are well aware of its value. A drawing by Mr. Mallows (Fig. 173) shows, next below a raised terrace, two square garden courts, the terrace steps between them descending to a long green walk, with flower-borders backed by yew hedges, leading to a circular fountain court paved and brick-walled. The perspective and plan of a garden by Mr. Inigo Triggs (Figs. 174 and 175) show the same need and good use of yew hedges for enclosing and protecting rectangular gardens. At Bulwick (Fig. 176) some old yews are clipped only where their lateral advance threatens the closing of a green path. Yew hedges have much use besides for securing privacy. Fig. 177 shows a young hedge that will be allowed to grow some feet higher to screen the offices and their possibly unsightly adjuncts from the pleasure garden. Such hedges are usually carried up to a height of from six to seven feet. For finishing the top the best-looking and most practical form is that of a very low-pitched roof ; this also presents the most easily accessible shape for clipping.

FIG. 171.—A QUIET BOWLING GREEN.

Though yew is undoubtedly the best tree for garden hedges, it is by no means the only one. Where the soil contains lime, or, in fact, in any good loam, the green tree box makes a fine hedge and clips well. But it is slow to grow—slower than yew—and both are costly. Ilex can be trained and clipped into tall hedges ; there are fine examples at the remarkably beautiful and successful Italian gardens at Brockenhurst. Green holly is also a fine hedge plant, but wants more width if it is to be carried up any height. For a quicker hedge at less cost there is the Lawson cypress, growing fast and clipping well. The humbler privet we all know ; it is quite cheap and soon grows into a neat hedge. We are so well used to seeing it bearing green leaves all the year that we forget that it is really deciduous. When it grows wild as a small twiggy tree it is leafless in winter. It is the trimming that induces

FIG. 172.—YEW HEDGE AS A BACKGROUND TO FLOWERS.

FIG. 173.—YEW HEDGES IN A DESIGN BY MR. MALLOWS.

FIG. 174.—YEW-HEDGED GARDEN BY MR. INIGO TRIGGS : PERSPECTIVE.

the fresh growth and leafing at an unusual season. Quite a pictorial effect is often seen of well-trimmed privet forming a sheltering entrance arch over a c o t t a g e door. Hedges of common laurel are so easily grown and so often misused that unthinkingly one has come to hold them cheap in estimation and to under-value their real merit ; but a laurel hedge twelve feet high is a splendid thing ; the size of leaf telling well in proportion to the height. It must be cut by hand ; never mutilated with shears, which would cut across the leaves. A tall hedge of bay is also a most satisfying sight, for the leaf itself and the whole growth are of a beauty and dignity that are

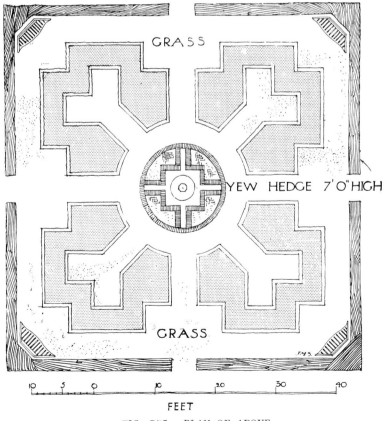

FIG. 175.—PLAN OF ABOVE.

FIG. 176.—YEWS AT BULWICK.

FIG. 177.—YEW HEDGE SCREENING OFFICES FROM GARDEN.

FIG. 178.—HEDGE OF PORTUGAL LAUREL BACKING A POOL GARDEN.

FIG. 179.—HEDGE CUT INTO LITTLE GABLES.

quite unequalled. This also must be cut by hand and the surface allowed a little freedom. Fig. 178 shows a hedge of Portugal laurel backing a lily pool in a good piece of rectangular gardening, and Fig. 180 a clever way of using pollarded and clipped limes for greatly heightening a garden wall abutting on a road.

For commoner purposes, such as a hedge to a kitchen garden, beech and horn-beam are both excellent. They serve also, especially hornbeam, for training over arbours and covered ways; growing close and twiggy when regularly clipped.

All such green hedges must be well planted, the ground deeply d u g a n d liberally e n r i c h e d a n d, i f possible, further encouraged during the next few years by additions o f m a n u r e just under the surface. T h e y cannot be hurried. Nothing is more frequent or more fatal t h a n compliance with the wish of the im-patient client who desires to have an effect at once. It can only be success-fully done by special and unusual means and at great cost. For yew and holly, three feet is the limit of height for prudent planting. Beech can be planted four feet to five feet high at o n c e ; hornbeam, privet and white-thorn should be cut down to within a few inches of the ground

FIG. 180.—POLLARDED LIMES USED TO HEIGHTEN A WALL.

the year after they are established, when they soon throw up a number of strong shoots.

Besides the green things used as actual hedges, fine effects are gained by the use of upright trees bounding grassy walks. Fig. 182 shows Lombardy poplars so used by Mr. Reginald Blomfield. Irish yews, the upright cypresses and their near relations, the junipers, can be so employed. Of the junipers, the neat

FIG. 181.—TOPIARY WORK AT MATHERN.

Chinese and the much larger Virginian—commonly called red cedar—are the best. Topiary work, to which the yew is so submissive, is receiving attention in modern gardens.   As in the case of other toy-like tricks in gardening, it may in some cases be satisfactorily employed, but if followed merely as a fashion, and not because the design of the garden would be bettered by a certain form, it may easily give an impression of silliness or wanton frivolity.   But fine effects are sometimes gained, where there is need for distinct punctuation, by carrying up a square plinth some six inches or eight inches above the level of the top of the hedge and growing a well-formed ball upon that.   Fig. 181 shows yew hedges at Mathern with the trees, at important points, trained up in the form of swollen cones surmounted by bird forms.   In unpractised hands such treatment might be dangerous, but in that of Mathern's owner we know that his skill and fine taste will bring them into right and fitting garden ornaments.

FIG. 182.—A GARDEN AVENUE OF LOMBARDY POPLARS.

CHAPTER XIV—WATER IN THE FORMAL GARDEN.

" The Soul of Gardens "—Reflections—Pools and their Water-levels—Varied Shapes—
Lily Ponds and their Depth—Separate Pool Gardens—Water Parterres—Fountains
and their Sculpture—Leadwork—Well-heads—Pumps.

" FOUNTAINS and waters are the soul of gardens ; they make their chief ornament and enliven and revive them. How often it is that a garden, beautiful though it be, will seem sad and dreary and lacking in one of its most gracious features, if it has no water." So wrote Pierre Husson in *La Theorie et la Pratique du Jardinage* in 1711, and set down a truth that is coming into its own again. This chapter is called " Water in the Formal Garden " because it is concerned with water as a factor in design, rather than as the element which makes possible all the enchanting growths proper to the water garden in its technical meaning. Husson, who published his book in Holland, had all the French devotion to rather theatrical uses of water. He extols " eaux jaillissantes, celles qui s'élevent en l'air au milieu des bassins, forment des jets, des gerbes, des bouillons d'eaux." Appropriate as such features are in great gardens, water needs to be employed very simply in small ones. Little pools and rills and fountains, with their waters not too vigorously " jaillissantes," need to be disposed with a sparing hand.

Although the gardens at Hurtwood, Surrey, are of large extent when taken together, the great variation in levels necessitated their division into several gardens, some quite small, which are complete in themselves, and therefore useful to illustrate our argument. Even in the great fan garden, the features at the radial point from

FIG. 183.—FAN-SHAPED LILY POOL AT HURTWOOD.

FIG. 184.—HURTWOOD: RELATION OF STEPS AND POOL.

FIG. 185.—FOUNTAIN WITH BASIN AND OBLONG LILY POOLS AT HURTWOOD.

which it starts, *i.e.*, the fan-shaped pool and paved work, give suggestions for the treatment of quite small gardens. The result of the delightful design made by Mr. Christopher Turnor for Major - General Sartorius, V.C., appears in Figs. 183 and 184. The chief pool is fan-shaped, and thus leaves between the water and

FIG. 186.—AT GREAT BADDOW : REFLECTIONS.

FIG. 187.—HURTWOOD : LOOKING DOWN ON FOUNTAIN.

the open parapet a half-round space which gives hospitality to flowers. The paving is well managed. The stones which edge the water are of regular shape, while the rest of the space has random flagging. Near by is another pool, which, by throwing out a curved edge to meet the chief flight of steps, marks a

FIG. 188.—PARAPETTED POOL AT BLYTHBURGH.

FIG. 189.—POOL IN PAVED COURT.

FIG. 190.—AT MORTON HOUSE, HATFIELD.

happy relationship in design between itself and the stairways from the higher ground. No less ingenious is the treatment of the garden on the west side of the house (Figs. 185 and 187, and for plan see Fig. 98). Water here also takes a prominent place. A round basin is set on a square base built of tiles with a stone coping. From the basin rises a fountain with its figure spouting freshness. On each side of this central feature is an oblong lily pool, and the whole design is bound together by a broad frame of paving.

Simple pools, with the water brought up nearly to the ground-level, give a pleasant variety to a paved court when it is enclosed by the wings of a house built on

FIG. 191.—SHAPED POOL AT ATHELHAMPTON.

an H plan. This is well shown in a design by Mr. C. E. Mallows (Fig. 189). His drawing suggests what is one of the chief charms of pools, however small. Since Narcissus first espied his face in a fountain, wise designers of gardens have been mindful of the beauty of reflections. Whether it be a window, as in Mr. Mallows' drawing, or vase, yew and dovecote, as in the parapetted pool at Blythburgh in the garden of Mr. Seymour Lucas, R.A., or the little boy's figure and the garden-house at The Vineyards, Great Baddow (see Figs. 186 and 188)

FIG. 192.—AT WOOTTON LODGE, STAFFORDSHIRE.

FIG. 193.—SMALL POOL AND NICHE AT ATHELHAMPTON.

there is a changeful beauty in the dim outlines and fleeting colours of reflected things that no other element in garden design can give. In order to ensure these effects it is important that the water should be kept at its proper level, which is as high as is possible. The nearer it is to the kerb of the pool, the wider and more beautiful will be the reflections. Nothing looks more dreary

FIG. 194.—IN A PETERSFIELD GARDEN.

FIG. 195.—AT ISLAND, STEEP.

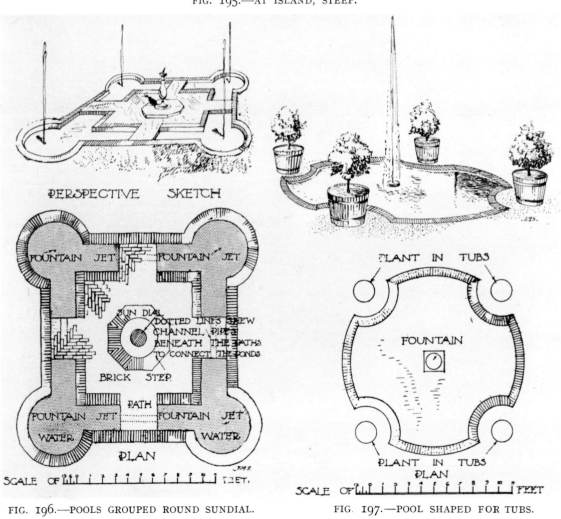

FIG. 196.—POOLS GROUPED ROUND SUNDIAL.   FIG. 197.—POOL SHAPED FOR TUBS.

than a tank of three or four feet in depth with only a few inches of water in the bottom, the more so as its walls are apt to be slimy. When water is scarce in rainless seasons this may be unavoidable, but there is little excuse for a permanently low level, which is

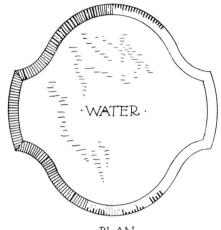

PLAN
SCALE OF FEET

FIG. 198.—A SIMPLE SHAPE.

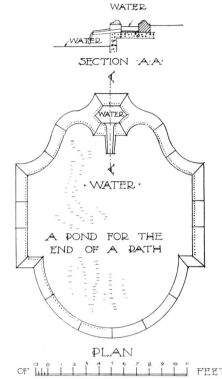

WATER

SECTION ·A·A·

·WATER·

A POND FOR THE
END OF A PATH

PLAN
OF FEET

FIG. 199.—WITH RAISED INLET.

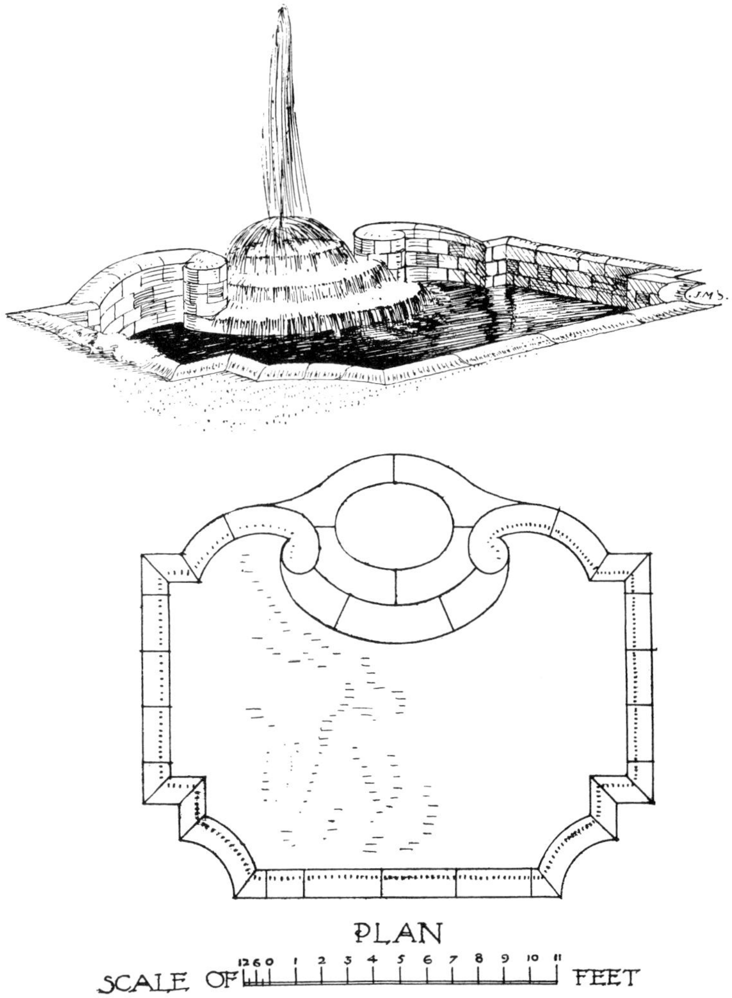

PLAN
SCALE OF FEET

FIG. 200.—WITH JET AND CASCADE.

usually the result of placing the inlet and outlet too low in the wall of the pool. At Morton House, Hatfield, Mr. A. Winter Rose has set in a paved court a round pool which groups pleasantly with the loggia and a statue in its niche (Fig. 190). The shapes which garden pools can take are almost endless in their possible variety, but it is usually well to be satisfied with simple forms. The illustrations of this chapter show rectangles in various proportions, which are generally dictated by the paved court or grass plat in which they are set. Two types of oblongs with curved ends are illustrated, from the gardens of Wootton Lodge, Staffordshire, and

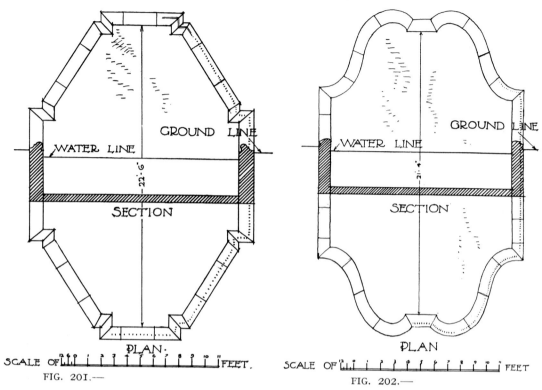

WATER LINE

GROUND LINE

22' 6"

SECTION

PLAN.

SCALE OF FEET.

FIG. 201.—

WATER LINE

GROUND LINE

SECTION

PLAN

SCALE OF FEET

FIG. 202.—

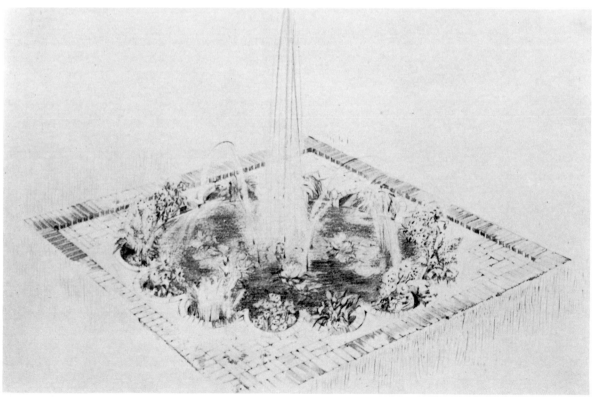

FIG. 203.—POOL AND FOUNTAIN DESIGN BY MR. H. INIGO TRIGGS.

Athelhampton Hall, Dorset. Of the two the former (Fig. 192) has a slightly more broken outline, and is given an increased architectural emphasis by the moulding of the raised kerb. The latter (Fig. 191) is as simply made as can be, save that a rounded moulding overhangs the side of the pool a little. It should be noted that the axial line of this feature cuts through the middle of the gate to the walled garden in which it is, and the full effect of water treatment in helping an interesting vista is thus secured.

Another little pool, fan-shaped, in the same garden is illustrated in Fig. 193 to show how well it groups with the niche in the wall above it. The possible

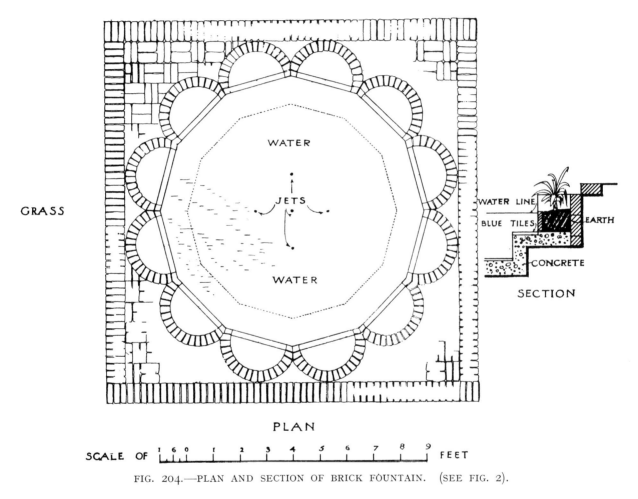

PLAN

SCALE OF ⌐ 1 6 0   1   2   3   4   5   6   7   8   9 ⌐ FEET

FIG. 204.—PLAN AND SECTION OF BRICK FOUNTAIN. (SEE FIG. 2).

combinations of pools with other features are well-nigh endless, and it is not possible to show more than a few typical examples. A very attractive treatment is shown in Fig. 194, where the drop in level from one terrace to another is made the occasion for an amusing little stepped bridge of masonry. This was designed by Mr. W. F. Unsworth and Mr. Inigo Triggs for a garden at Petersfield, and very successful it is. To the same architects is due the manipulation of simple elements in a garden at Island, Steep (Fig. 195). A double flight of steps leads down from a long upper terrace to a lower one, which juts out over the hillside with a semi-circular bastion-like front. The curve of the stairs determined the outline of one end of the pool, and the similar

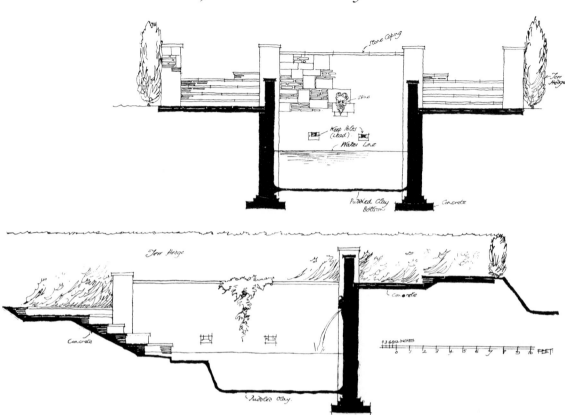

FIG. 205.—CROSS AND LONGITUDINAL SECTIONS THROUGH LILY POND, MILLFIELD.

FIG. 206.—LILY POND AT MILLFIELD, BRENTWOOD.

FIG. 207.—SMALL POOLS INTERSPERSED IN PAVING.

shape of the other end marches with the plan of the lower terrace. The chief purpose of this pool, as of most of its kind, was to find a home for water-lilies. Surrounding the basin, and less than a foot below the normal water-level, is a shelf about fifteen inches wide, on which may be set pans or baskets containing lily plants. There are varieties which, on account of their intrinsic value, or for the purpose of ensuring better growth, it is desirable to place in this way. It may be added that some of the more robust water-lilies will grow in from six to ten feet of water, but such a shelf as is now described need never be more than two feet below the ordinary level,

FIG. 208.—SUNK POOL GARDEN AT MARSH COURT.

and is more convenient if only about six inches below. A practical point worth remembering in the construction of such pools is the risk they bring to those gardens that are made the more gracious by the presence of little children. If they are built with broad, shallow steps which drop by gentle degrees towards the middle of the pool, an over-venturesome child is not likely to come to very serious harm. The gradually receding levels of the stone or brick, moreover, add to the appearance of the pool, when the water is clear enough to reveal its floor. In Figs. 196 to 202 are shown seven pool shapes drawn by Mr. J. Maxwell Scott from sketch designs by

FIG. 209.—POOL, STEPS AND BALUSTRADE.

FIG. 210.—AT PAPILLON HALL.

Mr. Inigo Triggs. Four are simple outlines, and one of them is devised to leave suitable spaces for the placing of pots of shrubs. Fig. 196 provides a quartette of connected pools grouped round a baluster sundial. Another is furnished with a jet and a little stepped cascade. The example shown in Fig. 199 is designed to come at the end of a path, and has a little raised basin from which the water spouts into the pool.

Although very simple forms are the safest for pools, there is room for an occasional burst of gaiety in outline, especially when the rest of the garden plan is of necessity treated in a severe fashion. The brick-edged pool shown by plan and perspective in Figs. 203 and 204 was designed by Mr. Inigo Triggs, and is reminiscent of the wealth of fancy that enlivens the gardens of the East. The jets are very happily placed ; they would make a garden so

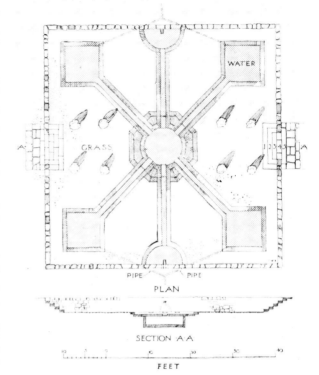

FIG. 211.—PLAN OF WATER PARTERRE.

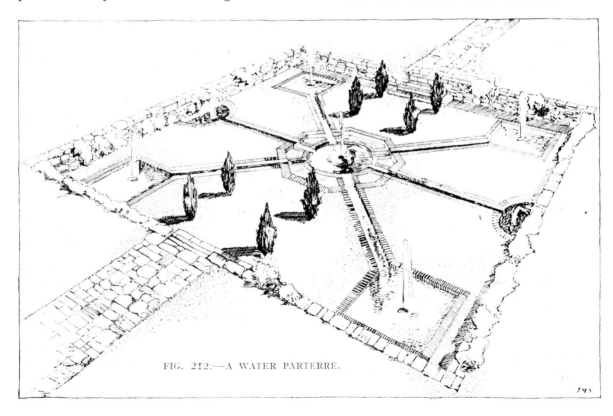

FIG. 212.—A WATER PARTERRE.

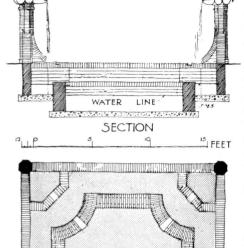

WATER LINE

SECTION

12 0   5   10   15 FEET

PLAN

adorned a little Paradise of freshness, and musical with the tinkle of falling spray. In Figs. 205 and 206 are illustrated by sectional drawings and photograph an attractive stepped lily pond at Millfield, Brentwood, designed by Mr. A. Winter Rose. The parapetted walls add considerably to its effect. The interspersing of many little pools tied together by a coherent geometrical design in a long stretch of paving is another treatment of water which is of large interest, as is shown by Fig. 207. There is a suggestion of patches of enamel set in ivory.

Water takes its highest place in garden architecture when it determines the complete design of an enclosed space, such as the pool garden at Marsh Court, devised by Mr. Lutyens, and illustrated in Figs. 208 and 209. No scheme contrived within so small a compass could exceed in richness of effect this combination of steps, paving, pool and balustrade. A note of gaiety is added by the lead hippocampi, to the modelling of which reference is made later (see Fig. 221). In the same manner, but on a smaller scale, is the delightful pool at Papillon Hall (Fig. 210), where

FIG. 213 —WALLED POOL WITH ANGLE FOUNTAINS.

the contrast between the curves of the descending steps and the lines of the margin of the pool is altogether successful.

Another scheme of design, eminently suited to gardens of limited area, is the water parterre, such as is shown by plan and perspective by Mr. Inigo Triggs (Figs. 211 and 212). The design, made by the same hand, for a walled pool and fountains, reproduced in Fig. 213, is unusual and interesting. The water is carried to shaped basins on the top of brick piers at the four corners, whence it falls into tanks built in the corners of the dwarf walls. As designed, there is no provision for an entrance to the little path that runs round between the dwarf wall and the kerb of the pool, and if the design were carried out in this way, the water would run across a rough channel in

FIG. 214.—EXTENDED POOL AT CHELWOOD VETCHERY.

the path on its way to the tank. If, however, it were desired to make an entrance-way to the enclosure, it would be desirable to carry the water through the corner tanks to the main tank by a pipe embedded in the path. This treatment is intended for a flat site, so that the level of the kerb of the pool and its adjacent path would be the same as the surrounding garden. On this basis the height of the dwarf wall would be no more than eighteen inches, the total space occupied being only a square seventeen feet six inches each way. It should be added that tall fountains of this type can only be worked in connection with a supply cistern placed at a higher level than the basins.

The shaped pool at Chelwood Vetchery, designed by Mr. Rome Guthrie (Fig. 214), is part of a large and imposing scheme of garden design ; but it is instructive as showing an idea equally applicable on a smaller scale. The pool is placed below the retaining

FIG. 215.—TILE-BUILT FOUNTAIN BY MR. LUTYENS.

wall of the terrace (the curved projections of which are also worthy of attention), and the sense of length is emphasised by the extension of the pool as a narrow canal. This is an interesting variation of the canal or rill treatment, which is also shown in the Berkshire garden (Fig. 21) and at Little Boarhunt (Fig. 67).

The design of standing fountains is generally the outcome of combining two elements—a basin and some sculptured fancy that discharges the water. The various types of pools illustrated in this chapter are capable of being supplemented by little spouting figures, such as are illustrated in Chapter XIX., which is concerned with statues. The *Boy and Dolphin* shown there would look well, for example, in a pool like that of Fig. 191. Smaller conceits, however, take an attractive place on tanks of limited size. In Fig. 217 is shown the section of a simple round basin, for which Lady Chance modelled a very attractive tortoise, cast in lead (Fig. 218), and some toads. Other examples of fountain sculpture by the same skilful hand are the hippocampus of Fig. 221 and the lion mask of Fig. 216. The latter is for a wall fountain discharging into a bowl built up in tilework

FIG. 216.—LION MASK FOR FOUNTAIN.

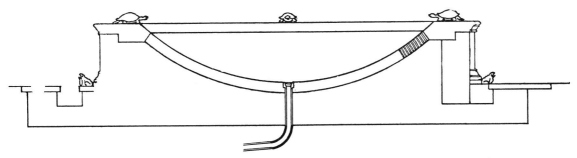

FIG. 217.—SECTION OF BASIN WITH LEAD TORTOISES ON RIM.

(Fig. 215), designed by Mr. Lutyens. The hippocampus is a delightful beast, spouting from his muzzle, and was used in a group of four disposed symmetrically on the

FIG. 218.—LEAD TORTOISE BY LADY CHANCE.

outer margin of the rectangular tank at Marsh Court (Figs. 208 and 209). In all these examples the sculptor has shown her felicitous sense of the right treatment of animal forms. She has shown, for example, not an exact representation of a tortoise, but an interpretation of one,

FIG. 219.—LEAD DOLPHIN.

FIG. 220.—GARGOYLE FOR GARDEN WALL.

bringing to her work that just quality of convention which makes it art instead of naturalistic imitation. Another pleasant lead spout for a garden fountain is the

FIG. 221.—HIPPOCAMPUS IN LEAD.

dolphin modelled by Mr. Cashmore, and illustrated in Fig. 219. The gargoyle designed by Mr. Voysey, and built up in sheet lead, serves a rather different purpose (Fig. 220). It is fixed to the front of a big brick retaining wall at Littleholme, Guildford (see also Fig. 102), and has a delightfully grotesque quality that is suggestive of the mediæval craftsman. Its purpose is to throw clear of the wall the surface water drained from the terrace above.

A combination of pool with wall fountain which is singularly attractive is to be seen at Hampton Court (Fig. 223). The entwined dolphins spouting freshness into a big shell owe no little to their intrinsic charm as sculpture, and modern replicas would, no doubt, be of greater cost than the owners of most small gardens could encompass, but their placing with reference to the twin pools below is very happy and suggestive. Though the atmosphere of gardens does not demand that their ornaments shall be great sculpture, it occasionally happens that a master hand models a figure that finds its way into a garden setting. The slender fountain at Wych Cross Place, illustrated in Fig. 222, is a case in point, for it is the work of that great but erratic sculptor, Alfred Gilbert. The bronze stem was modelled for some altogether different purpose. Upon it has been set a simple old Dutch bowl of stone, and to crown the composition, the exquisite statuette by Gilbert of a *Dancing Boy*, stung by a fly and holding a tragic mask in his hand It is very successful, and the figure has that enchanting vitality which makes it reasonable to call Gilbert the English Carpeaux. It is characteristic of the casual, fragmentary career of this great artist that the bronze stem should have lain unheeded in a dealer's shop until the owner of Wych Cross Place found for it a use so admirable.

Among modern fountains made wholly of lead a high place must be given to the composition shown in Fig. 224. It consists of an octagonal tank, decorated in flat relief with grapes and vine leaves, combined with a tall fountain, in which its designer and maker, Mr. George P. Bankart, has gone for inspiration to a late mediæval example in the South Kensington Museum. The treatment of the metal is exactly right ; the modelling is softly done, and the corona at the top of the fountain is in openwork of lace-like effect to which lead lends itself so well. Simpler and smaller tanks than this are very helpful in the water equipment of any garden. Eighteenth century tanks, such as that illustrated in Fig. 229, are

FIG. 222.—BY ALFRED GILBERT.

FIG. 223.—WALL FOUNTAIN AT HAMPTON COURT.

FIG. 224.—LEAD TANK AND FOUNTAIN.

not difficult to acquire. The areas of old London houses continually disgorge examples with panelled fronts that bear dates and initials and little classical devices of all kinds. The modern craftsman, however, should not be forgotten in the ruling passion for " antiques." Two examples by Mr. Bankart are illustrated in Figs. 225 and 226. One of them, with its stout swag of fruit and flowers, has a definite garden character, and the other has delicate ornament in slight relief which suits well the nature of the material. When cisterns like these for convenience in watering the garden are remembered, the needs of the birds must not be

FIG. 225.—LEAD CISTERN.

FIG. 226.—BY MR. GEORGE BANKART.

FIG. 227.—CHALICE BIRD BATH.

forgotten. Fig. 228 shows a shallow bird bath made of lead, and Fig. 227 a chalice-shaped vessel of terra-cotta, both admirable in their different fashions.

There are few small gardens that can boast a stream or an old moat, but either is a welcome feature, for it gives opportunity for a bridge. Illustrations elsewhere in this book (*e.g.*, Figs. 21 and 194),

FIG. 228.—SHALLOW BIRD BATH OF LEAD.

show how effectively bridges can be contrived in connection with pools, and the problem of a little stream is not greatly different in kind. In the little garden at Kelsale Manor, Saxmundham, there is an old and narrow moat, over which Mr. A. Winter Rose has thrown a little oak bridge, which is shown in Fig. 230. Over a continuation of this moat is a small stone bridge by a curved stairway (Fig. 231). It forms a connecting link between the lawn and the parkland beyond.

Most of the pools illustrated in this chapter are designed on definitely formal lines, and it is only rarely that naturalistic treatment produces satisfactory results. When, however, a cottage has been set on a rough hillside and the heather reaches to the door, a conscious garden scheme may be undesirable or even impossible. Such is the case at Stoneywell Cottage in Charnwood Forest (Fig. 232), where the margin of the bathing-pool has been made to follow the natural contour of the ground. Mr. Ernest Gimson has shown a just

FIG. 229.—A GOOD XVIII. CENTURY TANK.

FIG. 230.—A LITTLE WOODEN BRIDGE.

FIG. 231 —AT KELSALE MANOR.

appreciation of the character of the site by making the pool accord in its rough simplicity with the attractive, roughly-built cottage which it serves, and with the pump-house, which also appears in the picture.

On the subject of well-heads a note of warning may be sounded. Where an actual well exists it is very desirable that its head should be made an attractive thing. The modern example illustrated in Fig. 234 has a simple stone wall and coping with a wrought-iron "overthrow" of neat design. Most people, however, who are set on possessing a well-head look for an old one. There seems no end to the stream of them, old or "antique," which does not necessarily mean the same thing in these days of skilful reproduction. They come, or are said to come, from Italian courtyards and gardens, some complete with the old iron arching that

FIG. 232.—BATHING POOL AT STONEYWELL COTTAGE.

holds the pail-hook and supports a pulley. Heads which are carved of grey and other dark-hued stones are more suitable for English gardens than those of white marble, which are apt to look harsh and staring. Many of them are adorned with the arms of families represented now in Italy by nothing but the memory of their names

FIG. 233.—OF ISTRIAN STONE.

FIG. 234.—A MODERN WELL-HEAD.

FIG. 235.—ITALIAN WELL-HEAD WITH "OVERTHROW."

and the bravely-carved heraldic achievements on a well-head. One of the two old examples in Istrian stone illustrated in Figs. 233 and 235 once belonged to the Marcello family, now extinct. The other is ornamented with simple and appropriate representations of a water vessel. Such memorials of a grandiose world which has not survived the clash of modern life may be well enough in a great English garden. For the smaller schemes of design, for which we are now considering the appropriate type of ornament, they are less fitted than a well-head built of brick or stone. It is, however, in their placing that most care is needed. The example at Sutton Courtenay (Fig. 238) stands well on its broad spread of paving, but very often one is seen set down on a grass plat without any suitable base, and looking lonely and useless. There is no reason why a well-head should not be used as a dipping-well or fitted with a jet and used for a fountain in a pool. Such a use renews its connection with water, but to employ it as a flower-pot is an indiscretion. Not to employ it at all, but to regard it merely as an ornament, seems justified only when it has marked merits as a piece of sculpture. The fact remains that Italian well-heads are appropriate in Italy and sometimes look awkward in an English garden, especially when they are not used in connection with a well, which rarely exists in a place where decorative emphasis is possible or desirable.

FIG. 236.—A WOODEN PUMP CASING.

Figures 236, 237 and 239 are concerned with the more typical English water engine, the pump. In the eighteenth century pump - heads were commonly made of lead and decorated with little lion masks, rosettes and dates. Fig. 237 shows a good example, but placed as it is it lacks meaning and looks uncomfortable. It is rather difficult but possible to adjust such a pump-head to the mechanism of a modern pump, and that method seems the only reasonable one to adopt. An interesting alternative is suggested by the foreign pump casing of wood (Fig. 236), panelled and carved, now preserved in the South Kensington Museum. The iron handle is delightfully wrought, and the general effect suggests that here is a field for decorative effort. There are many gardens which rely for their watering on roof water, bath wastes, etc., carefully gathered and conducted to an underground cistern which needs to be pumped for garden use. In such a case it is good to have an attractive rather than a merely utilitarian pump. This wood-cased example may therefore be helpful in suggesting a covering treatment for the modern pump of commerce.

FIG 237.—LEAD PUMP-HEAD.

It sometimes happens that the well is close to the house, and occupies a prominent place in the garden. In such a case it is good to make a virtue of a necessity and use the well as an opportunity for an interesting architectural feature. In Fig. 239 is shown a well and pump-house at Pitsford, which Mr. Morley Horder has treated attractively. The roof space serves as a pigeon-cote.

It is hoped that this chapter may give a stimulus to the use of water in the formal garden. Its employment as a decorative element fell into great neglect during the Victorian period, and is even now imperfectly understood. It is true that it took an important place in some of the big gardens which owed their design to such men

FIG. 238.—AT SUTTON COURTENAY.

as Sir Joseph Paxton, but it was not very wisely employed.   As early as 1821 Paxton made a large lake at Battlesden Park, where he was employed as gardener, and he was responsible for the great fountains at Chatsworth.   The work of his school, however, showed no sound appreciation of the possibilities of water.   The lessons of Versailles and Hampton Court had been wasted as far as the nineteenth century was concerned.   Especially was this the case in the use of water as an element in the design of small gardens.   The qualities that make for successful treatment of limited spaces are the same in principle as in the case of big areas ; the differences are only in detail.

We need not be so dogmatic as Bernard Palissy, the great French potter of the sixteenth century, who wrote :   " It is impossible to have a spot proper for a garden unless there be some fountain or stream passing through it."   Nevertheless, our illustrations show how great an aid water brings to the designer of gardens, and with water companies spreading their mains far into country districts, much can be done without the ideal means of a natural stream.

FIG. 239.—PUMP-HOUSE AT PITSFORD.

CHAPTER XV.—METHODS OF PAVING.

Rectangular Jointing—Random Jointing—Local Methods—Pitched Paving—Paving of Shingle—of Brick and Tile.

IN some portions of the garden, and especially near the house, some kind of paving is sure to be wanted. Where a suitable local stone exists, it is, of course, the best thing that can be used, although the style of the house may be a determining influence in the choice of the material. Thus, a house of eighteenth century character or a garden of formal design seems to demand a pavement of squared flags of York or Portland stone (Fig. 243), while a house of the cottage class may be content with random-jointed stone, or even with a few rough-edged flat slabs laid like stepping-stones through grass and flowers, to give a dry footway to a modest entrance (Fig. 242). Stones of the Yorkshire class, and also those related to slate, present smooth surfaces by natural cleavage, and are the most suitable for using as rectangular flags— there is something distasteful about laying them with "random" joints. It is sometimes done, but always has a displeasing appearance, whereas such treatment is unobjectionable in the rougher-surfaced sandstones.

Some of the most interesting methods of paving are those that are peculiar to a district—that grow directly out of the employment of some local product that has stimulated inventive use from past ages. There are a few square miles in West Surrey where the hard sandstone called Bargate stone is quarried. A quite different kind of stone, largely composed of iron, also occurs in small pieces close to the ground-level. Many of these, weather-washed for ages, are of a form that presents one or two sides or ends with a flat surface. A typical stone would be three to four inches

FIG. 240.—A SUMMER-HOUSE PAVING OF IRONSTONE AND BARGATE STONE.

FIG. 241.—PAVING SIMPLY TREATED WITH STONES OF NATURAL SHAPE.

in length, an inch wide and three inches deep. For hundreds of years they have been used by the country people, set on edge, as a "pitched" paving, often with a deeper kerb of the hard sandstone. Whole inn-yards may be found of such pavement. Sometimes they were set in patterns and are so used now, with guiding lines of the yellowish sandstone and a filling of the purplish black ironstone. Fig. 240 shows such a

FIG. 242.—ROUGH-EDGED SLABS.

FIG. 243.—PAVEMENT OF RECTANGULAR FLAGS OF PORTLAND STONE.

FIG. 244 —STONE PAVING WITH " RANDOM " JOINTS.

FIG. 245.—A CIRCULAR AND CONCENTRIC BRICK PAVING.

FIG. 246.—PAVING JOINTED TO FOLLOW THE TERRACE PLAN.

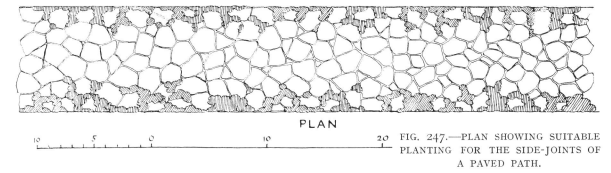

PLAN

FIG. 247.—PLAN SHOWING SUITABLE
PLANTING FOR THE SIDE-JOINTS OF
A PAVED PATH.

FIG. 248.—PAVEMENT OF RECTANGULAR FLAGS IN A ROSE GARDEN BY MR. GILBERT FRASER AND
MR. T. H. MAWSON.

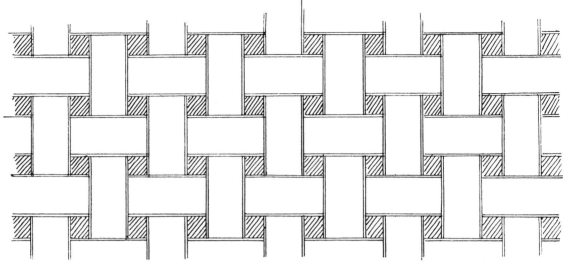

FIG. 249.—AN OLD SUSSEX CHURCH PAVING OF BRICK.

FIG. 250.—PAVEMENT RATHER OVER-PLANTED IN THE MIDDLE.

pavement as the floor of a summer-house.

In the case of places near the sea, pretty pavings can be made by collecting stones of different colours from among banks of shingle. There is hardly a shingle beach that does not contain stones that are nearly black and nearly white, and others with several shades of buff and brown, only waiting for the invention and ingenuity that will work them into patterned pavements.

When it is not convenient or desirable to use stone there is the alternative of brick and tile, materials which also offer a wide field for thoughtful and clever treatment. The circular paving round the sundial (Fig. 245) shows how ordinary paving bricks may be laid, without any shaping of the bricks, in a way that is extremely simple and yet full of dignity. A radiating pavement of tile and brick can also be made of roofing tile on edge forming the rays with a herring-bone filling of brick. A pavement under

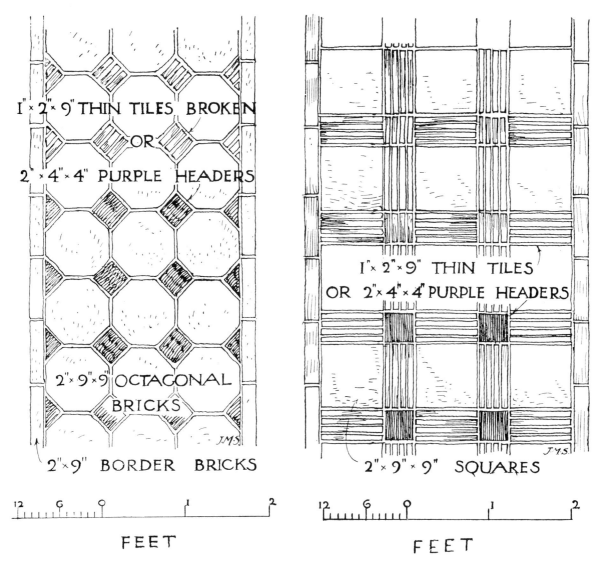

1" × 2" × 9" THIN TILES BROKEN

OR

2" × 4" × 4" PURPLE HEADERS

2" × 9" × 9" OCTAGONAL BRICKS

2" × 9" BORDER BRICKS

1" × 2" × 9" THIN TILES OR 2" × 4" × 4" PURPLE HEADERS

2" × 9" × 9" SQUARES

FEET

FEET

FIG. 251.—BRICK AND TILE PAVING.

FIG. 252.—BRICK AND TILE PAVING.

the pergola at Marsh Court (Fig. 263) of large stone flags, with filling of brick, is simple and stately. In more than one old church in Sussex there is a paving of red brick set in a pattern that suggests interwoven ribbons (Fig. 249). The small dark squares were specially prepared by bricks of the usual size, having the surface deeply channelled in the mould so as to form eight divisions. These bricks were then "flare-burnt," the surface acquiring a purple colour and half vitrified quality, while the deep scoring made them easy to cut into the small squares. Paving bricks are also moulded to special patterns, as with one end diamond-pointed for the fitting of four ends together, as in Fig. 254, the square inter-spaces being filled with nine-inch tiles. Fig. 253 shows an example of a tracery of sections of half-round tile connected with small pieces of roofing tile, with filling of another material, and Figs. 251 and 252 illustrate various ways of using pieces of roofing tile and brick on edge with paving tiles of square and octagonal form.

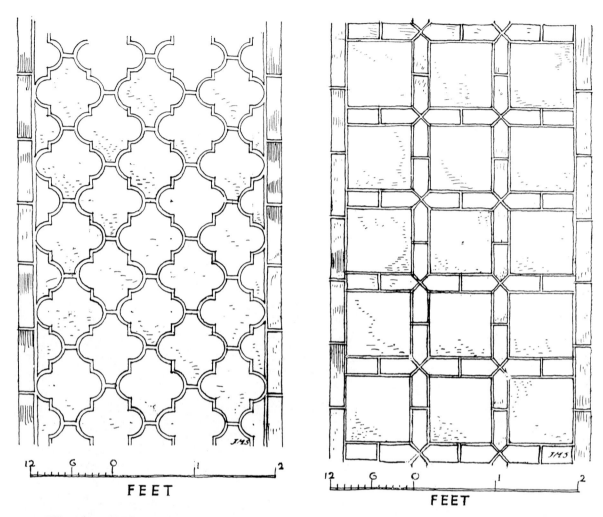

FIG. 253.—BRICK AND TILE PAVING.   FIG. 254.—BRICK AND TILE PAVING.

Any person of inventive capacity and some skill in handicraft can make delightful pavements with tesseræ of pieces of broken roofing tiles. The tesseræ are prepared by cutting the pieces of tile into small cubes of approximately the same size with a cold chisel and hammer; they are then set to the pattern desired in mortar or cement on a concrete bed prepared beforehand, and brought up to a suitable level.

CHAPTER XVI.—THE PERGOLA.

*Italian Pergolas—English, of Oak—Of Larch Poles—With Stone, Brick and Tile Piers—
Proportions—Garlands on Chains—Suitable Plants—Covered Alleys—Treillage.*

WHEN one considers how commonly some kind of pergola is used in Italy, it
would seem a matter for wonder that it has taken so long to reach us in
England, for twenty years ago it had hardly been thought of. But now
it is a familiar garden feature, and, translating its original use as a convenient means
of growing vines and ripening grapes into our English way of having it for the
display of beautiful climbing plants, as well as for its comfort as a shady way in
summer, its development for our needs has of late years been surprisingly rapid.
In fact, so popular has it become that there is scarcely an example of modern garden
design in which it does not
find a place. It is true that
it is often injudiciously placed.
There are many gardens that
have not had the benefit of
experienced advice, where a
poorly - constructed pergola
stands in some open place where
it has no obvious beginning or
end ; whereas it should always
lead from one definite point
to another ; one at least being
some kind of full-stop, either
of summer-house or arbour,
or, at any rate, something of
definite value in the garden
design.

As to construction, we
follow in the main the Italian
prototypes. In many cases
the pergola is a mere framework of poles (as shown in
Fig. 255), replaced from year
to year, either wholly or in
part as the need arises, or it
has posts of solid masonry.
These are commonly built of
rubble, thickly covered with
that lime plaster of coarse
texture that is so well used
by Italian masons. These
columns are sometimes square,
but more often round in

FIG. 255.—A PERGOLA OF POLES IN VENICE.

FIG. 256.—PIERS OF RUBBLE, PLASTERED, AT AMALFI.

section (Fig. 256). In some cases even, marble pillars from some ruined ancient building are brought into use—always with a satisfying effect of solidity and permanence.

When in our British gardens there can be no question of such solid treatment and only rough wood is available, the posts of the pergola are best made of oak trunks of anything from eight inches to ten inches diameter. Their lifetime can be lengthened by stripping the bark off the butts for a length of three feet and coating the stripped part with gas-tar. Charring in the fire is even better, but is less convenient to do in the case of heavy posts. It is important that the tarring or charring should be carried to a height of quite a foot clear of the ground, the danger-spot being at the ground-line and just above it. The oak posts being set up, a rather slighter log, adzed at the ends on what is to be the under side (so as to lie flat and steady), is spiked to each pair of posts across the path, any slight curvature of the

FIG. 257.—LARCH PERGOLA OF TOO SLIGHT A CONSTRUCTION.

log being taken advantage of to show some degree of upward camber. Nothing looks weaker or less satisfactory than a cross-beam that swags downwards, as it does naturally when of weak stuff, or if not adzed at the ends to give a firm seat. This weak effect shows in the larch pergola illustrated in Fig. 257, which is altogether too slight in construction. Pergolas of this class often show such cross-beams of weak, drooping form, and stiff, straight braces cut out of the larch tops. The braces are better when shaped as in the picture of the pergola with a paved path and fir trees at the end (Fig. 258), where they are cut out of branches that have a little upward curve.

The example built of larch poles supporting gourds is cleverly done, the braces of alternate posts taking a wide angle, and, after passing and being spiked to the beam, joining at a ridge point ; the wider angle helps to give more rigidity to a flimsy structure and the prolongation affords more spacious support to the shoots of the gourds (Fig. 259) Often a house and garden are occupied on a short tenancy, such as three years ; in this case such a pergola of short lifetime would form a delightful feature.

When it is possible to build with solid piers, we see how thoroughly our architects and garden designers have assimilated the pergola idea, and the many and various ways in which they are working it out and adapting it for combination with other structures. In the example at St. Clere, Kemsing (Fig. 260), designed by Mr. Godfrey Pinkerton, it covers a wide flagged terrace adjoining one side of the racquet court. The piers are built of large, flat paving tiles resting on a stone step, and have stone caps and bases. They carry a heavy, continuous beam; lesser beams, with one end resting on this, have their other ends treated putlog fashion and built into the house wall. A singularly satisfactory pergola by Mr. Inigo Triggs (Fig. 261) is built of ordinary brick with wide mortar joint, on short plinths of rough local stone, with steps of the same. Oak timbers

FIG. 258.—OF LARCH POLES WITH WELL-SHAPED BRACES.

from an old building form the roof. Chains hang from post to post for the future training of roses as garlands. In a very beautiful open pergola at Marsh Court, designed by Mr. Lutyens (Fig. 263), the piers are built of tiles with wide joints ; they have stone plinths and moulded stone caps, the section being square and concave square alternately. This fine example also shows the value of the solid, slightly cambered beam. In some cases a good effect is gained by building the piers round and square alternately (Fig. 264). It is not difficult to have bricks specially moulded for building in the circular form. At Home Place, Norfolk (Fig. 265), a clever use is made of cobble stones by Mr. E. S. Prior, where four round cobble piers are set four-square on a circular platform raised on two steps, which forms the centre of wide, flagged, radiating paths. A good effect is gained, and might be more often obtained in build-

FIG. 259.—GOURDS ON LARCH FRAMEWORK.

ing generally, by not filling up the putlog holes. A fruit-room at Chelwood Vetchery, five sides of an octagon in plan, is happily treated by Mr. Rome

FIG. 260.—A WELL-BUILT PERGOLA ADJOINING RACQUET COURT AT ST. CLERE.

FIG. 261.—PIERS OF BRICK AND STONE.

FIG. 262.—A PERGOLA WITH PIERS, SOME ROUND, SOME SQUARE.

Guthrie, with a surrounding pergola following the same plan (Fig. 266). The piers are circular in section, of a light-coloured brick, and stand upon a flagged platform. The whole is planted with vines, the most beautiful of all pergola plants.

Brick piers at the ends, with wooden ones between, and a roofing of trellis over a brick pavement, form a pergola at Sandhouse, Sandhills, Witley (Fig. 267), from the design of Mr. F. W. Troup. This pergola is unusually high in proportion to its width. It is in general more agreeable to let the width across the path be greater than the height, as in the example by Mr. Walter Cave at Ewelme Down, where some specimens of topiary work in tubs are placed at the ends of paths (Fig. 268).

FIG. 263.—PIERS OF TILES, WIDE-JOINTED.

A pergola of open structure by Mr. J. P. White at Garston Park gives partial shelter to a garden door. Under it is a wide, flagged terrace, slightly sloping away from the house to throw off rain, the joints near the planted piers being left open for the benefit of the climbers. Against the house is an interesting reproduction of the old-fashioned perspective treillage (Fig. 269).

For a general guide as to dimensions, it may be taken that the piers may be anything from seven feet two inches to eight feet out of the ground, eight feet to nine feet apart across the paths, and nine feet to twelve feet apart in the length of

FIG. 264.—ALTERNATE ROUND AND SQUARE PIERS.

FIG. 265.—A MEETING-PLACE OF RADIATING PATHS.

FIG. 266.—A PERGOLA SURROUNDING A FRUIT-ROOM.

the path. It is often a convenience, especially in the case of wooden posts, to have the roofing of flat iron arches ; but in this case it is well to fasten some kind of wooden rods or slight trellis to the iron, the contact with cold iron in winter tending to check and damage some plants. When chains hang from post to post to form garlands, it is also well to wind a tarred cord rather closely round the chain, so that the shoots rest on the cord and not on the chain. But a better way is to have two chains spread apart about six inches with rigid iron ties, for the training to this is more under control. All gardeners who have had to do with rose garlands know the trouble of the whole thing swinging round to the under side, like a saddle turning on a horse.

In some large gardens iron pergolas have been adapted for the growing of pears and apples trained as cordons (Figs. 270 and 271). They are formed of successive arches, all in one piece, of thick iron rod, with wires fastened longitudinally. They form a pleasant as well as interesting shady path, and, as the trees are necessarily pruned to short spurs, the quantity of bloom is a wonderful sight in proportion to the space.

As a general rule, the pergola is most satisfactory when on level ground, and when it is straight from end to end ; but it is sometimes convenient for it to follow flights of steps and landings leading from one level to another. Such a case has been cleverly treated at Acremead in Kent (Figs. 272 and 273), to the design of Mr. Dunbar Smith and Mr. Cecil Brewer, where it goes straight downhill, with solid square piers of local stone. Easy flights of steps and landings give access

FIG. 267.—AT SANDHOUSE.

to paths at right angles. As to the best plants for pergolas, there is nothing more delightful than grape vines, or for other good foliage aristolochia and Virginia creeper. Where flowering plants are desired, there are wistaria, clematis, and preferably the kinds near the species such as *montana*, *Flammula* and *Vitalba*, white jasmine, Japan honeysuckle, Dutch honeysuckle (both of the early and late kinds), *Bignonia radicans* and climbing roses. But roses on pergolas need great care in regulating by pruning and training, their inclination being to run up to the top,

FIG. 268.—AT EWELME DOWN.

FIG. 269.—A PERGOLA SHELTERING A GARDEN DOOR.

FIG. 270.—A PERGOLA OF CORDON FRUIT TREES.

FIG. 271.—OUTER VIEW OF THE FRUIT PERGOLA.

so that unless the pergola is on a lower terrace and is seen from above, the beauty of the mass of bloom is lost. There are also a number of shrubs and small trees that can be adapted for pergola use, one of the best being laburnum. At West Dean in Sussex there is a complete tunnel of laburnum with an ivy arch at the two ends (Fig. 275). Among other shrubs that can be trained to the same use are guelder roses, *Pyrus Malus floribunda*, snowy mespilus, laurustinus, common laurel, *Solanum crispum* and *Robinia hispida*.

The pleached alleys of our Tudor ancestors have much in common with the pergola. Columns, arches and whole galleries of shady verdure, trained on a foundation of wooden treillage, are described by Bacon. They were commonly planted with hornbeam or wych elm. Treillage was also used to a large extent in French gardens in the eighteenth century, but it is only now that it is being revived in England. In Fig. 274 is shown an example by Mr. J. P. White with walls, arbours and rose temples.

There is still earlier record of something of the pergola kind in England, for in

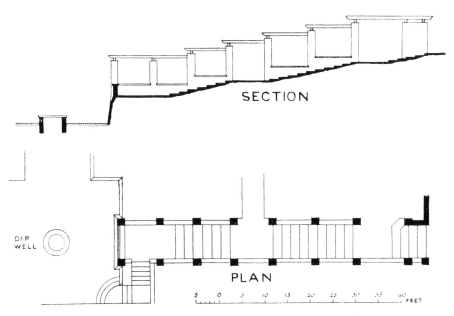

FIG. 272.—AT ACREMEAD: PLAN AND SECTION.

FIG. 273.—STEPPED PERGOLA AT ACREMEAD.

FIG. 274.—A GARDEN OF TREILLAGE.

William Horman's "Vulgaria," published in 1519, nearly a century earlier than the works of Bacon, these passages occur : "Aleys in gardens covered with Vynes and railed up with wythe stakis vaute wyse do great pleasure with the shadowe in parchynge heat." And further : "A vyne clevynge to his railes with his twyndynge stringis and lette hangynge down his clusters of grapis maketh a plesaunt walkynge aley."

FIG. 275.—A GREEN TUNNEL OF LABURNUM.

CHAPTER XVII.—GATES AND GATEWAYS.

Entrance Stairways—Gates to Forecourts—Carriage Gates—Notes on Eighteenth Century Smiths—Gateways and Vistas—In Walled Gardens—Wooden Gates.

BOTH before and since Robinson Crusoe "made up the Entrance, which till now I had left open," the treatment of the way into house and garden has been fruitful of varied opportunity. Crusoe was concerned for the safety of his house and gear, and had an eye to those same needs of defence that find such delightful architectural expression in moat and bridge, gatehouse and portcullis. The small house and garden, however, raise no such military problems, and the possibilities are limited to the treatment of archways in high walls, gates that break the line of low walls and sometimes the provision of steps. In Fig. 276 is shown an

FIG. 276.—GATE AND MOUNTING BLOCK AT CLEEVE PRIOR.

FIG. 277.—AT BIDDESTONE MANOR.

attractive pair of wooden gates approached
by two curved steps. Beyond them a
mounting block witnesses to the days before
petrol had all but supplanted horseman-
ship. The entrance to Biddestone Manor
(Fig. 277) shows the good effect of a simple
and well-designed pair of stone piers and
a longer flight of steps. The battery of
Time and lichen have left their tender
marks on this typical Cotswold ashlar-
work. When the house is close to a
frequented road it ensures a larger privacy
if the wall is carried high and the doorway
made in an arched opening, as in the
example designed by Mr. Walter Brierley,
and shown in Fig. 279. A sense of security
is given by filling the tympanum of the

FIG. 278.—GATEWAY TO A COURTYARD.

FIG. 279.—ENTRANCE FROM ROAD TO SMALL GARDEN.

arch with wrought-iron work, and the
gate is the easier to open from not being
the full width of the opening. A similar
treatment is shown in Fig. 278, where an
iron gate gives entrance to a paved
courtyard.

The steady increase in the use of
motor-cars by people of moderate means
tends to make a carriage entrance
necessary for houses of quite modest
size. Many are content with the provision of a simple field gate; but when
something more ambitious is contemplated,
the design of the gates themselves and of

the adjoining walls is a serious factor in the artistic success of the house and its approach. The disposition of the entrance to a Berkshire house designed by Mr. W. J. Parker is somewhat ambitious in scale, but its plan shows a treatment appropriate to small houses if carried out on smaller lines. From the brick piers at the ends of the boundary walls the line of the wall curves inwards to the piers of the carriage gates (Fig. 280). In these curved wings on

FIG. 280.—TREATMENT OF WALL AND GATES.

either side of the main carriage gates (Fig. 281) are set two foot-gates and two round grilles (Figs. 282 and 283), all of which gave pleasant opportunity for the art of the modern smith. The wise choice of iron gates of good design has considerable bearing on the successful appearance of an entrance. So many eighteenth century houses in towns are now being demolished that old gates can often be acquired at reasonable prices, and the chance of finding one is worth enquiry and some little trouble; but caution is necessary. Old gates are not worth buying unless they are in a satisfactory condition, because repairs to them are apt to cost almost as much as new gates. Moreover, it is a mistake to be led into buying a gate, however pleasant its design, if it is not of the right size and proportion for the opening that needs to be filled. The writer of this bears in mind an unhappy friend. Ten years ago he bought a gate and stretch of railing of admirable design and in good repair, in the hope that it would "fit in somewhere," but he has never contrived a place for it. The methods of the "bargain sale" do not apply conveniently to architecture. It may be helpful, however, to set down notes on some typical work of the old smiths, in order to show the sort of work which is good and pleasant, whether it be old or new. Fig. 285 shows a delightful gate of the size suitable for the entrance of a small country house. It is fixed in a wall between two gardens, and never served as a carriage gate, for there is insufficient head-room under the "overthrow," but in character of treatment it is very instructive. It was made in 1720,

FIG. 281.—THE CARRIAGE GATES.

and is traditionally believed to be the work of the Brothers Roberts. The character of the work supports the tradition. The year 1719 is the earliest that can be associated with the independent activities of the Roberts, for they then did the very elaborate gates at Chirk Castle. They do not seem to have worked much outside Shropshire, Cheshire and Wales.

FIG. 282.—GRILLE IN SCREENWALL.

FIG. 284.—VISTA BETWEEN TWO GATES IN WALLED
GARDEN.

FIG. 283.—FOOT-GATE.

Leeswood, near Mold, Emral, Eaton Hall and Shrewsbury were among the places that boasted notable examples from their smithy. The design of the gate illustrated in Fig. 285 is the best guide to its attribution. No one could have made it in 1720 who had not fallen under the spell of Tijou or at least of his book of designs. The horizontal lines are heavily emphasised and the embossed shells at the top of the side panels are unusually prominent. The "overthrow" of the gate is very marked by the range of embossed acanthus leaves (derived apparently from Tijou's gadroon and acanthus border) which connect the two stout horizontals supporting the pyramid of scrollwork, etc. A rather unusual feature is the trio of oval rings at the base of each side panel. The embossed leaves are well executed, though without the natural swirl that characterises them in Tijou's work and connects them organically with the iron tendrils to which they are fixed. For all that, their placing in the design is very happily managed, and could not have been done by a smith who knew nothing of Tijou's pioneer work. The execution is very good, and the repairs which Mr. C. G. Hare has lately superintended fortunately did not need to be extensive. No doubt the succeeding owners of the gate have been careful to keep the ironwork painted. Without such attention the slight substance of the embossed work would long since have rusted away. Modern craftsmen doing similar leafwork commonly use sheet copper or sheet bronze, which defies the weather and can be blacked as easily as sheet iron.

The history of English wrought-iron gates can hardly be said to have begun until the advent of Jean Tijou in 1689. Further particulars of the career of this great artist are given in a chapter (by Mr. J. Starkie Gardner) in *The House and*

FIG. 285.—GARDEN GATE MADE BY THE BROTHERS ROBERTS.

its Equipment. Tijou's influence was not, however, universal. Without him English smiths
would probably have continued to make strong
gates and railings of straightforward design, with
little fancy ; but it is unlikely that they would
have adopted the repoussé work which is so
characteristic of Tijou. His influence is clearly
shown in the delightful gate at Wotton House
(Fig. 287). Despite the obvious attractions of the
new methods, the national liking for a large restraint
in craftsmanship persisted even under the very eye
of Tijou. While he was working at St. Paul's some
less important commissions in the Cathedral were
entrusted to Thomas Robinson, who was evidently
an individualist, for he did not follow at all closely

FIG. 286.—AT WYCH CROSS PLACE.

in Tijou's steps. Where he
used embossing it was with
imperfect understanding of its
possibilities. When he was free
from the master's influence
and began working at New
College, Oxford, about 1711,
he discarded the Tijou style
and developed a simpler manner
of his own which is markedly
English. Warren and (despite
his Dutch-sounding n a m e)
Buncker did work of a similar
kind during the first quarter
of the eighteenth century. The
gates at Packwood House,
Birmingham (Fig. 288), and at
Norton Conyers (Fig. 289), show
this more restrained note in
design, the latter in a marked
degree.

The majority of the gates
of the first half of the eighteenth

FIG. 287.—AT WOTTON HOUSE

FIG. 288.—AT PACKWOOD HOUSE, BIRMINGHAM.

century—the golden age of the English smith—are of this simple type. Embossed work is used sparingly, and the basis of their designs is scrolled work taking the form of lyres and G's, variously combined and enriched by water-leaves. Occasionally there is a diversion into naturalesque forms, when terminals spread out as bunches of laurel leaves. What may be called the London type was essentially sober, though rich in treatment, and it is this type which should be followed in the entrance and garden gates of the small modern house. They should be built of stout bars. Satisfactory results cannot be got from flimsy sections, and the temptation to use light material to save cost is to be resisted. Far better a simple gate of adequate sections than one bedecked with acanthus but lacking strength.

FIG. 289.—AT NORTON CONYERS.

Where there is a garden-house approached by a long walk with an opening in the wall at the end of it, as at Norton Conyers (Fig. 289), it is permissible that the gate should be of less sturdy build, so that the full value of the distant picture be not lessened. Another example of this is seen in the very light gate in a wall that divides two long paths at Wych Cross Place (Fig. 286).

Considerable space has been given to historical notes on the design of iron gates because so many garden pictures are spoiled by ugly examples, but the placing of the gates is an even more important question. When Fleming wrote in 1576: " It

FIG. 290.—AT WITTERSHAM HOUSE.

was my happy chance to have entrance into a goodly gardene plotte," he unfortunately did not say what manner of gate let him in, but we may imagine it was at the end of a long alley such as the Elizabethans loved. In the planning of gardens the gates of walled enclosures can often be placed on axial lines, so that the full value of a vista may be secured. The gateways illustrated in Fig. 284 show this well.

Walled gardens are especially favourable to

FIG. 291.—AT GREAT MAYTHAM: MAIN GATE TO WALLED GARDEN.

interesting gate treatment, as may be seen in Figs. 291 and 292, which show examples at Great Maytham designed by Mr. Lutyens. The larger gate is the chief, and the smaller a subsidiary entrance to the same garden. By the same hand, but on a much smaller scale, is a little gateway in the garden of Wittersham House (Fig. 290). The outlines of the ironwork are of the simplest, but the gate has the quiet distinction which follows good design even on the smallest scale and in the humblest materials.

Although the chief place of gates will always be at the entrance to carriage-ways and in walled gardens, a long terrace some-times gives opportunity, as at Chelwood Vetchery, the seat of Sir Stuart Samuel, Bart., M.P. Mr. Rome Guthrie has here marked a drop in terrace level by an iron gate between brick piers at the head of a flight of steps curved on plan.

In Fig. 284 is shown a good pattern of wooden garden gate, made of stout

FIG. 292.—IN THE WALLED GARDEN AT GREAT MAYTHAM.

FIG. 293.—AT CHELWOOD VETCHERY.

FIG. 294.— WOODEN DOOR WITH POSTERN.

oak bars. Though itself modern, it is of earlier type than those of wrought iron which have been described. Sometimes for the sake of greater privacy a solid wooden door is desirable, as in the attractive old Tudor example with a postern which is illustrated in Fig. 294. Always satisfactory and with the added merit of being very inexpensive are doors of simple wood trellis, such as Mr. Lutyens has employed at Great Maytham (Fig. 295).

Not less important than the gates themselves are their posts. The Packwood House example (Fig. 288) is built in rusticated brickwork with a simple stepped top, but the eighteenth century was much addicted to ball finials, as at Norton Conyers (Fig. 289), and no better finish can be devised.   For smaller gates the treatment shown in Fig. 287 is admirable ; the steps in the wall make the upper part of the opening wide, and give opportunity for an overthrow of more imposing design than the width of the gate itself would allow. It is a happy compromise between a simple narrow gate and one with a pair of side panels running the full height, as at Norton Conyers (Fig. 289).

A word on the undue growth of creepers is never out of season. The wanton growth of ivy on the left gatepost in Fig. 288 shows how this noxious weed veils cornice mouldings and destroys architectural proportion and balance. In addition, there is to be remembered the deadly injury done by ivy shoots in penetrating and loosening the joints, until in an evil day it pulls down the fabric which has endured its baleful embrace.

Stairways of all kinds are considered in their proper chapter, but reference may be made here to the curved steps, built of brick on edge, which add so greatly to the charm of the gate at Packwood House (Fig. 288).

FIG. 295.—A TRELLIS DOOR.

CHAPTER XVIII.—GARDEN-HOUSES.

The Plan of Summer-houses in General Scheme—Building in Vernacular Manners—Thatched Roofs—Cob—Use of Old Materials—In Walled Gardens—Shelters and Tool-houses.

THE success of summer-houses and pavilions, considered as elements of garden design, depends as much upon their skilful placing as upon their form and materials. It may be laid down that, in cases where the pavilion is near the main house and related to it by path or pergola, it should have the same architectural treatment. By way of example we may refer to Fig. 296, which shows a design by Mr. H. Inigo Triggs. In this case the pavilion serves as a focus for the other elements of the design. It is connected with the house by a pergola, and its four windows overlook the lawn, the sunk garden, etc. It is proper, therefore, that it should be of the same half-timber construction as the house, to which it stands in a definite relation. It is an outpost where the amenities of the house and its more gentle employments can be enjoyed in a garden atmosphere. From the architectural point of view it is an added value in such a pavilion that it gives dignity and scale to the main building. This is notably the case at

FIG. 296.—A GARDEN-HOUSE DESIGNED BY MR. INIGO TRIGGS.

FIG. 298.—AT HURTWOOD: GARDEN-HOUSE ABOVE LILY POOL.

Hurtwood (Fig. 298), where the simple gazebo at the corner of the terrace emphasises the height of the house behind, and serves as a pleasant resting-place whence the beauties of the outlook may be enjoyed. Its situation above the lily pool helps to mark the charms arising from the wise treatment of a site that slopes

FIG. 297.—GARDEN-HOUSE AT ATHEL-HAMPTON.

sharply. Similar advantage has been taken of a difference in level between two important sections of a garden at Athel-hampton (Fig. 297), where the windows of the pavilion command both an upper lawn and a long vista of path and border on the low side of a clipped hedge. Where a forecourt or terrace has been built up on a hillside, a corner gazebo, like that shown in Fig. 299, designed by Mr. Walter Cave, seems to buttress the terrace, while it serves as a delightful vantage-point whence the country round may be espied. The quality to be aimed at in all garden architecture is coherence in the relationship of parts. A pavilion should not stand alone, but be tied to the rest of the scheme by orderly design. Where the house is of definitely classic form, it is permissible that the summer-houses shall take on the aspect of a little temple. In Mr. Arnold Mitchell's garden at Great Baddow, illustrated in Fig. 300, the vista made by path and borders is

FIG. 299.—GAZEBO AT CORNER OF TERRACED FORECOURT.

FIG. 300 —AT THE END OF A LONG WALK.

closed by a pleasant little classical conceit in stone. In the case of houses of no marked style, it is better for the design of pavilions to follow the vernacular traditions of simple building proper to various districts.

A garden at Liphook shows the pleasant results of rough masonry and tiles employed in two summer - houses designed by Mr. W. T. A. T. Carter (Figs. 301 and 302). One has a hexagonal roof in the corner of the wall; the other is of L plan, which marks the end of

FIG. 301.—AN ANGLE SUMMER-HOUSE NEAR LIPHOOK—

FIG. 302.—AND ANOTHER OF UNUSUAL PLAN.

the wall, and has a delightful little conical roof rising at the angle. This unusual and interesting plan has the practical advantage that the occupants of the pavilion have two views, one down the path to the first summer-house, the other across the lawn. Reference must also be made to the treatment of the wall. The stepping in its parapet is emphasised by the crowning of the piers by simple ornaments of obelisk type which have quite a Jacobean flavour. But they are no more than old rick-stones, and their mushroom-shaped tops have been placed under the stalks to serve as bases. It was an ingenious thought to give these old features of the farmyard a new lease of life as garden decorations. At The Grove, Mill Hill, Mr. Stanley Hamp has designed a pleasant garden - house (Fig. 303) in brick and timber, which is the more interesting for

FIG. 303.—AT THE GROVE, MILL HILL.

FIG. 304.—THATCHED HOUSE IN NORFOLK.

being set on the side of a sharp slope. Rising as it does from a well-grown herbaceous border, it dominates its surroundings in very agreeable fashion, and looks across a wide stretch of garden to the house, with which it accords well.

The thatched pavilion at Happisburgh, Norfolk, designed by Mr. Detmar Blow, is in a vernacular manner (Fig. 304). The house which it adjoins is also thatched. In general this roof treatment needs to be employed with discretion. Sometimes a rustic pavilion, log-built and thatched, will be placed in relation to a house

FIG. 305.—THATCHED SUMMER-HOUSE IN ANGLE OF COB WALLS.

of some definite architectural period, such as Georgian, and only succeeds in creating the idea that its builder is playing at rusticity. When, however, a summer-house is placed in a remote corner of a garden and bears no definite relation to the main house, some latitude is permissible. Nothing could be more attractive than the Devonshire example illustrated in Fig. 305, where a thatched summer-house shelters in the corner of a walled garden. In this case the walls are built of "cob," *i.e.*, of earth rammed

FIG. 306.—AT LITTLE BOARHUNT, LIPHOOK.

in the local fashion, which has prevailed for centuries. A cob wall (or *pisé*, as it used to be called early in the nineteenth century) will last almost for ever, if it is built on a stout foundation of stone or brick or concrete, and if it is soundly roofed with thatch, so that the wet is kept from its sole and its head. Where the natural treatment of the adjoining wall is thatching, it is wholly fitting that the summer-house should be roofed in the same fashion. The solecism to be avoided is the importation into a part of the country, where thatch is unknown, of a ready-made thatched pavilion framed in barked logs, which are too often made garish and ridiculous by yellow varnish.

FIG. 307.—BUILT OF OLD MATERIALS.

The use of old materials—of the *disjecta membra* of demolished buildings — is a piece of amateur antiquarianism which needs to be approached with some reserve. There are cases, however, where an old set of columns will take their places faithfully and naturally as the supports of a new-built garden-house. Such a use is illustrated in Fig. 307. It is the more appropriate because this

FIG. 308.—OF TWO STOREYS.

delightful curved pavilion, with the tiles well " swept " in the making of its conical roof, adorns the garden of an old house in Broadway, where a ripe age gives the prevailing atmosphere. A pavilion built up of ill-assorted Elizabethan fragments may, however, look very uncomfortable in a garden which owes its design wholly to the eighteenth century. In the gardens of small new houses it is far safer to accept modernity as the governing factor, and to build a garden-house that frankly expresses the age to which it belongs. That is not to say that the teachings of historical design should be neglected. The garden-house at Little Boarhunt (Fig. 306) shows how satisfactory can be a pavilion which is not a copy of any particular old example, though it owes its pleasant aspect to a knowledge of what was

FIG. 309.—ROUND GARDEN-HOUSE AT LITTLE RIDGE.

done by the old builders. The round pavilion, shown in Fig. 309, stands at the corner of the formal garden at Little Ridge, laid out by Mr. Detmar Blow and Mr. Fernand Billerey, and is of characteristic and interesting design. Elliptical arches rest on its stout piers, and above the cornice the roof, ogee in section, rises to a pretty ball finial. A simple and attractive round summer-house at the end of a grass walk at Wittersham is shown in Fig. 312.

A good treatment of a garden-house in the

FIG. 310.—IN CORNER OF WALLED GARDEN.

corner of a walled garden is seen at Great Maytham, designed by Mr. Lutyens (Fig. 310). Though the scale is small, the little pavilion is given an air of comely dignity by the few steps which lead up to its door, and there is a practical thought in this provision. It gives a view over the outer garden from the windows on the far side. Yet another idea for a pavilion in the corner of a walled garden is afforded

FIG. 311.—AT ST. CLERE.

FIG. 312.—AT WITTERSHAM HOUSE.

by the example designed by Mr. W. F. Unsworth and illustrated in Fig. 308. The house is of two storeys, and the upper floor is carried on stout oak posts. The undercroft serves as a store for garden implements, and the room above is reached by an outside staircase on the other side of the wall. Such a little apartment makes a quiet retreat for a writer, or an admirable room for a bachelor when the normal sleeping accommodation of the house has reached its elastic limit. A very important detail in the design of any garden-house, which is to serve as an outdoor room for reading and writing, is the window. It is not enough to rely on the light that comes through the opening of access. One window at least should be provided, and so placed that the light comes over the left shoulder of the writer. If such a window chances to face south-west or south, a light curtain over it will prevent the sunlight falling directly on book or manuscript. Attractive open summer-houses can often be contrived with little cost of building by taking advantage of an existing corner formed

FIG. 313.—ASHLAR WORK.

FIG. 314.—ON A TERRACE AT CHISLEHURST.

by a garden wall. The example at St. Clere (Fig. 311), designed by Mr. Godfrey Pinkerton, gives a hint as to how such a little rest-ing-place may be c o n t r i v e d. A dwarf wall with two columns, side wall and pent-house roof make up an attractive place. The low front wall has an advantage o v e r columns running to the ground-level ; or it helps to temper the cold airs of spring and autumn to t h e occupant.

FIG. 315.—A SIMPLE GARDEN SHELTER.

An architect has his greatest opportunity when the garden-house is an integral part of the design of a broad terrace adjoining the house, but this does not often arise in the case of s m a l l garden schemes. T w o examples are, h o w e v e r, illustrated. For a house at Chisle-hurst (not small, it must be con-f e s s e d), M r. Maurice Webb has designed a t e a-house with an open front. It l o o k s down a long stretch of terrace and com-municates w i t h the lawn below b y a stairway flanked by vase-topped piers. The pavilion and the

FIG. 316.—A SEEMLY TOOL-HOUSE.

adjoining balustrade are ashlar-built of Bath stone, and the roof is covered with the stone slates which are the crowning glory of Cotswold manor houses.

In Fig. 317 is illustrated a terrace pavilion with a roof of ogee outline which is typically Scottish. It groups delightfully with a house of austere eighteenth century character which was designed by William Adam, father of the famous brothers who left such an indelible mark on our national buildings.

Though this chapter deals chiefly with garden-houses of solid construction, one picture is given of a garden shelter designed by Mr. Basil Oliver on lines which slightly recall Chippendale's trellis manner (Fig. 315).

It is as well to bear in mind that the outlying parts of the garden devoted to its purely working hours should not be made unseemly by tool-houses roofed with corrugated iron. In Fig. 316 is illustrated an attractive building for this purpose with weather-boarded walls and tiled roof, designed by Mr. A. Winter Rose.

FIG. 317.—A TYPICAL SCOTTISH GARDEN PAVILION.

CHAPTER XIX.—STATUES AND VASES.

Their Especial Value in Small Gardens—Scarcity of Good Models—Professor Lethaby on Leaden Figures—On Gate-piers—Cupids—Pan—The Right Placing of Ornaments.

IT seems to be thought rather generally that ornaments, such as statues and fountains, find their just place only in great formal gardens like those of Wilton, Drayton, Melbourne or Wrest Park. Probably this feeling is a survival from the day when the formal garden itself was held in small esteem, or tolerated only when it helped to frame some great historic house. It may be admitted that ornaments need to be employed sparingly in small gardens, and that an undue liberality in their use calls up visions of the mason's yard, but therein is no reason for their neglect. Another cause that has made designers of gardens, whether amateur or professional, rather chary of resorting to them is the scarcity of good models small enough to be in scale with a little garden. It is the fact that small figures which are genuinely old are rarely met with in salerooms. Many of the available examples that pose, not very plausibly, as "antiques" are copies of very poor models, and are rejected as soon as seen. Present taste has accepted the principle of formality in garden design. So far from formal treatment being suitable for great gardens only, it seems to be peculiarly applicable to little spaces. Where a garden scheme extends over several acres a designer can afford to be severely simple in the details of his conception. A broad grass walk which runs a hundred yards between herbaceous borders of, say, fifteen feet in width is a thing so delightful in itself that its charm is self-contained. The absence of a statue framed in clipped yews to close the vista is forgotten in the beauty of the wide sweeps of turf and blossom. Variety of growth and changeful schemes of colour provide the necessary incident. A little garden, however,

FIG. 318.—ON GATE-PIER.

FIG. 319.—BOY FIGURE IN NICHE AT END OF GRASS WALK.

if too simply treated, soon exhausts our curiosity. The more the designer lacks space, the apter should he be in making us forget his garden's limitations. Ingenious plea-santries of treatment here and there arrest the interest. By concentrating it they make the visitor oblivious of the smallness of the theatre which yields so much diversion. This is not a plea for many orna-ments, still less for any one that stands out markedly from its surroundings ; no more is claimed than that ornament of the right kind is even more welcome in small gardens than in big. It is admittedly diffi-cult to get anything small enough in scale that is at the same time pleasant as sculp-ture in its own right. There are always available little re-productions in bronze of the exquisite *Narcissus* at Naples.

FIGS. 320 AND 321.—ON GATE-PIERS AT PAPILLON HALL.

FIG. 322.—BOY AND DOLPHIN IN POOL.

It figures in a score of gardens, and always looks well. It is, however, unreasonable always to demand of a garden figure that it should be fine as sculpture.

Professor Lethaby wrote years ago of garden figures : "Lead is homely and ordinary and not too good to receive the *graffiti* of lovers' knots, red letter dates and initals." This theory must be withheld from such younger sons of the house as own pen-knives, but it shows a right attitude to such pleasant unheroic sub-jects as may properly find their being enshrined in lead. It is an insult to submit a finely modelled bronze or marble figure to the changing assaults of the English climate and to the slow invasion of lichen. In a little garden the *motif* of the sporting child is always fresh. Fortunately, there are many skilful artists who have turned their hands to modelling boys, winged and wingless, busy with every sort of merry employment. A few are illustrated here, some old, some new. The youngster at Temple Dinsley (Fig. 318) who surveys us, shield in hand and rather soberly, raises a question as to the placing of statues. Nowhere do they look better or more reasonable than on the top of gate-piers. Their size seems less than when they are nearer to the eye-level, and from a practical point of view they are better than large open vases, which it may be difficult to keep supplied

FIG. 323.—A PIPING BOY.

FIG. 324.—MODELLED BY JAN VAN NOST.

with growing flowers. Best of all, they give a human welcoming quality to the forecourt over which they seem to preside. A very attractive pair is the leaden Youth and Maiden dressed in eighteenth century costume that nod and beckon to each other from neighbouring gate-piers at Papillon Hall (Figs. 320-1). They are only about four feet

FIG. 325.—QUARRELLING CUPIDS.   FIG. 326. —AT MELBOURNE, DERBYSHIRE.

high, and of a type suitable for comparatively small, though not for very small, gardens. They will be recognised as little cousins to the well-known Watteau-like Shepherd and Shepherdess who simper at each other in the solemn atmosphere of the South Kensington Museum.

Very serious students of art are urgent to tell us that sculpture has no right to represent violent action ; but even austere critics are inclined to relax these rules in the case of *amorini*. There is just the right degree of movement in the chubby boy who rides a dolphin (Fig. 322) and spreads a sail to the favouring breeze. Very pretty and thoughtful is the little piper (Fig. 323) who surveys his garden world from the low pier at the end of a dwarf wall. Both these are of to-day, modelled by the craftsmen of the Bromsgrove Guild, very much in the spirit of the figures at Wilton (Fig. 324) and Melbourne, Derbyshire (Figs. 325-6). These were made in lead at the beginning of the eighteenth century by Jan Van Nost, a Dutchman who came to England after William III. became King, and helped to establish here the Dutch manner of formal gardening. The Melbourne *amorini* form a dramatic sequence. The chubby pair fight for the possession of a garland, mishandle each other severely, but in the fourth group (not illustrated) seal their reconciliation with a kiss. Sir George Sitwell has written that " a pleasure-ground, however small, should have its presiding genius, its Nymph of flower-garden or grove or woodland or Naiad of the well . . . to give a personal interpretation to the forces of Nature . . . and for this reason sculpture in a garden is to be regarded not as an ornament, but almost as a necessity, as like that last touch of colour in a picture which sets the whole canvas in a flame." Figures look well in wall niches, as in the garden, designed by Mr. A. Winter Rose, which appears in Fig. 319. The kneeling *Boy with Dolphin*, which serves as a fountain in the pool at Wych Cross Place (Fig. 329) has beauty in its own right, for it was modelled by Puech, an artist who has added no little to the beauty of Paris by his monuments. None the less, it is in the reflections it casts on the still water, and in its judicious placing by Mr. Thomas Mawson in relation to the terrace steps, that no little of its charm resides. A like fancy is the *Cupid and Swan* of Fig. 328, which makes an ideal ornament for a pool.

Among the many subjects with which the old designers chose to people their gardens there is none which is so steadily successful as Pan. The Romans used his bust chiefly as a *Term* set on a diminishing pedestal, and it is in this form and from a modern model that Fig. 327 shows him. Lead holds indisputably first place as the material for garden ornaments in England; but it is apt to be expensive, and cement, if rightly used and coloured, makes a satisfactory substitute. There remains terra-cotta, which can be admirable if of quiet colouring and attractive texture; but the shiny red of some clays is hard and unpleasant. Some delightful garden pottery of subdued reds and greys is made by the Potter's Arts Guild at Compton, Surrey, the enterprise of

FIG. 327.—A TERMINAL PAN.

Mrs. G. F. Watts. The bird bath, illustrated in another chapter, is a good example of the service ceramics can do to the garden, and there are many satisfactory bowls to be had in the same material, modelled on simple lines and sparingly decorated with swags of fruit and the like simple devices.

The right placing of statues and vases is of as much importance as their intrinsic merit. What, for example, could be pleasanter than the flower-pot on an old millstone which ends a stone-flagged path (Fig. 330). In the background is seen the always welcome figure of Gian di Bologna's *Flying Mercury*, who seems here to have alighted on a sea of bloom. Both vases and statues are very well employed in adorning balustrades and stairways, as in the example illustrated in Fig. 331, at Sandhills Witley,

FIG. 328.—CUPID AND SWAN RISING FROM POOL.

FIG. 329.—FOUNTAIN FIGURE BY PUECH AT WYCH CROSS PLACE.

designed by Mr. F. W. Troup, where two leaden gods make music from vantage points afforded by the staircase piers.

Of the many types of vases that are available, it is impossible within the limits of this book to illustrate a series; but we can at least show some differing examples, each good in its own way and appropriate to various surroundings. The stately pot that is seen in Fig. 332 is one of the brilliant works ascribed to Jan Van Nost. It stands on a terrace at Hampton Court Palace, but is of moderate dimensions. It is suitable, therefore, to serve as

FIG. 330.—FLOWER-POT ON MILLSTONE AND MERCURY IN BACKGROUND.

the chief feature of a small garden of formal design, that frames a house of early eighteenth century character. Fortunately, it has been well reproduced and can be obtained. As Mr. Lethaby has written of it: "The little sitting figures (which form the handles), slight as they are, are charming in their pose; the folded arms and prettily-arranged hair give us a suggestion of life, which most of these things supposed to be in the classic taste lack." In quite another manner is the lead pot (Fig. 333) with a band of open ornament traced in bright

FIG. 331.—STATUES GUARDING STAIRWAY.

tinning, made by Mr. George P. Bankart. Two other lead tubs by the same hand are illustrated in Figs. 334 and 335. In one a hen and her chicken stand against a background of corn, and in the other the little

FIG. 333.—WITH TINNED ORNAMENT.

FIG. 332.—AT HAMPTON COURT.

FIG. 334.—BY GEORGE BANKART.

panels made by a network of rope moulding are filled by the inhabitants of a Noah's Ark. All three have the character of simple and straightforward craftsmanship, which marks them as fitting for the garden of a cottage.

FIG. 335.—FROM NOAH'S ARK.

CHAPTER XX.—SUNDIALS AND SEATS.

The Placing of Sundials—Various Simple Types—The Game of " Clocks "—Stone Seats and Their Setting—Wooden Chairs and Tables.

SUNDIALS, like other ornaments, depend more for their decorative success on their right placing than on their intrinsic merit as garden sculpture. A common fault is the lack of a suitable base. In Mr. W. Robinson's garden at Gravetye Manor there is a sundial of twisted baluster pattern designed by Sir Ernest George. It is set on a moulded square base, which rises from an octagonal platform (Fig. 336). Simple and slender as it is, it has an air of dignity by reason of being properly set. By way of contrast there is illustrated in Fig. 337 a sundial of pleasant and sturdy design, which looks lonely and neglected on a lawn, and bears no relation to the rest of the garden. It needs a stepped base of some sort to detach it from its surroundings. No little of the value of a sundial is the opportunity it affords to emphasise the central point at the junction of converging paths, as at Ditton Place, Balcombe (Fig. 338). The octagonal base makes a pleasant break between the round of the baluster and the shallow circular step which lifts it above the paving. It was designed by Mr. Horatio Porter. The more imposing the sundial itself, the more need is there for a dignified base. Of the many examples of the lead *Blackamoor* that English gardens can show, none is better supported than the example illustrated in Fig. 339. The four steps are adequate for the importance of this very interesting figure, which was sold freely in the beginning of the eighteenth century by Jan van Nost. Anyone who is interested in the history of this famous garden ornament may be referred for a full

FIG. 336.—SIMPLE SUNDIAL ON ADEQUATE BASE.

account of it to *English Leadwork: Its Art and History.* The next illustration (Fig. 341) shows an eighteenth century variation of the simple baluster treatment, with women's masks connected by festoons of drapery. This, again, is an example of an interesting pillar, which loses much of its possible effect by its lack of a proper base or platform and a margin of paving. At Marsh Court there is an example of to-day, designed by Mr. Lutyens, which is admirable for many reasons.

FIG. 337.—A GOOD SUNDIAL BADLY PLACED.

The octagonal stone seat from which it rises provides a dignified base, and the stone pillar, which carries the most modern and scientific form of dial, has a charming entasis. Recourse was made for its decoration to a byway of the leadworker's craft, viz., inlay. It was popular enough in the Middle Ages, but has since been neglected, save for the dreary purpose of making imperishable the lettering on tombstones. Bands of simple conventional ornament wind spirally up the column between diamonds, all of lead inlaid in matrices cut in the stone. The whole composition is interesting and unusual. Wholly of lead, except for the iron gnomon, is the sundial illustrated in Fig. 343. Made by Mr. George Bankart, it is a good example of what can be done with the most typically English metal (in the Middle Ages and later the Continent got much of its lead from us). Good use has been made of a simple device which has pleased many generations of plumbers since the Roman occupation of Britain — the rope-moulding—and the leaf-work round the base is pleasantly modelled. Round the top is cast one of those many legends about the flight of time which have exercised the ingenuity of rhymesters since sundials were first made. Another, and more delicately adjusted, kind of outdoor timepiece is illustrated in Fig. 344. Its combination of slender hoops is pretty in itself, and the column which carries it did more active garden service once. It is a stone roller retired from work in favour of the more manageable

FIG. 338.—AT DITTON PLACE, BALCOMBE.

FIG. 339.—THE "BLACKAMOOR" SUNDIAL.

sort that the ironfoundry supplies. Of markedly rustic type, yet successful, is the mushroom-like example at Plewland, Haslemere. It is made of two rough-dressed stones, that formed one of the posts of an old farm " rick-settle,"

FIG. 340.—MODERN SUNDIAL AT MARSH COURT.

FIG. 341.—AN EIGHTEENTH CENTURY TYPE.

set on an old millstone, which rises a little above the surrounding paving (Fig. 342). Of the dials themselves in their manifold forms, and of the gentle art of dialling, which used to be a needful part of a gentleman's education, this is no place to write. Nor need we fill a page with any of the hundreds of sundial mottoes, which have been printed often enough in scores of gossiping books about gardens. It may be added, however, that some garden-lovers think it wise to be content with a plain brick pillar and concentrate the interest on the dial and gnomon. In Fig. 345 is illustrated an example of bronze, in which a girl with daintily-modelled figure leans over and plays " clocks " with a dandelion. It is a pretty fancy

FIG. 342.—TWO ROUGH-DRESSED STONES.

FIG. 344.—AN OLD GARDEN ROLLER IN A NEW EMPLOYMENT.

to set upon a sundial, and none the less fitting to be used because the game seems to have come with the modern child. It is at least much less than a century since the first reference to the game of "clocks" appears in literature. There is no better

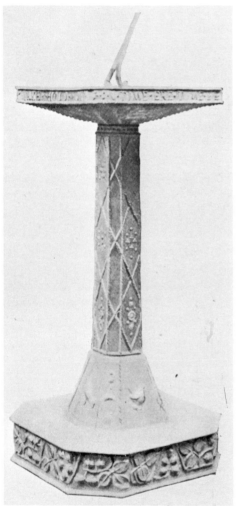

FIG. 343.—A LEAD SUNDIAL.

place for a sundial than in a rose garden, as at Marrowells, Walton-on-Thames (Fig. 346), designed by Mr. A. Winter Rose. In the middle stands the stone figure of a man. His head is bent over the sundial, which he holds to catch the rays of the westering sun. The hour of sunset is the time which chiefly brings out the beauties of a rose garden, and very admirable this statue looks as the late glow emphasises the strong modelling of the face, and an almost archaic simplicity in the heavy folds of the robe. The garden at The Vineyards, Great Baddow, shows a good example of a sundial placed on a circle paved with mingled brick and stone, radially set, which breaks a long gravel walk (Fig. 347). Another sundial which owes much of its charm to its setting on a broad expanse of circular brick paving is at Saighton Grange (See Chapter XV).

There is a certain reasonableness in grouping in one chapter " Sundials and Seats." In days of universal watches the function of the sundial is to be decorative

FIG. 345.—THE GAME OF " CLOCKS."

and to stimulate gentle moralising. For the latter employment the best authorities are agreed that it is well to be comfortable in body, not always an easy thing to be contrived in a garden. For sheer comfort there is no doubt that something of flimsy appearance, made of canvas and a few sticks or of basket-work, is best; but both

FIG. 346.—STATUE HOLDING DIAL IN ROSE GARDEN.

FIG. 347.—PLACED AT INTERSECTING PATHS.

FIG. 348.—AT SEDGWICK HALL, HORSHAM.

FIG. 349.—AT DANBY HALL, YORKSHIRE.

FIG. 350.—STONE SEAT DESIGNED BY MR. PETO.

FIG. 351.—AN ISOLATED SEAT.

FIG. 352.—SEATS AND TABLE IN APPROPRIATE SETTING.

kinds have the disadvantage of suffering in the weather. The seat that will defy the rain is therefore a necessity, but it is more—it is a decorative aid. In Fig. 350 is illustrated a carved stone seat designed by Mr. Peto. It comes at the end of a terrace, and with its gay little flanking figures closes the vista in delightful fashion. A stone seat never looks better than against a background of yew. This may be seen in a simple example at Sedgwick Hall (Fig. 348), and in another, of imposing classical aspect, at Danby Hall (Fig. 349.) It is always desirable for the builder of a stone seat to provide an adequate stretch of paving in front of it, which is the better, both practically and in appearance, for being raised step-height above the adjoining grass or gravel. It is not a good thing to place a seat in an isolated position, as in the example, well designed in itself, which appears in Fig. 351. A bench

FIG. 353.—DESIGNED BY MR. LUTYENS.

should give the impression of being there to be sat on, and that is not likely to be very convincing if there is no path to give access to it. In the majority of small gardens, however, it will be found more practicable to rely on movable wooden seats of stout build. Teak or oak are the best materials, but well-seasoned deals, of a sort that does not tend to split on

FIG. 354.—BY MR. J. P. WHITE.

exposure to rain and sun, are good enough if carefully and regularly painted. Green is a doubtful colour for a seat, as it is likely to quarrel with the varied natural greens which are near it. White is safe, but looks rather staring during the seasons when there is no brilliant colour in the flower garden to relieve it. Oak untreated and allowed to take on the silvery hues which weather will bring to it is, on the whole, the best

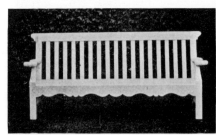

FIG. 355.—BY MR. J. P. WHITE.

material for the garden seat ; teak, though good, because almost everlasting, is not of so pleasant a colour.

It is well to provide a paved space for such heavy wooden furniture as is not likely to be moved about. Gravel is not comfortable for the feet, and the disadvantages of grass are obvious. An admirable arrangement at Wittersham House is shown in Fig. 352. Three long seats, two chairs and a table are arranged on a paved floor, and the wall behind is treated with niches holding basket-bearing lead boys between pilasters crowned by trophies of fruit. Flower vases standing at the corners of the paving complete a very pretty

FIG. 356.—DESIGNED BY MR. MAURICE WEBB.

FIG. 357.

FIG. 358.

scheme of an open-air room that must be a pleasant place for the discussion of tea. In Fig. 356 are shown a well-devised table curved on plan, and a pair of armchairs, designed by Mr. Maurice Webb, for the tea pavilion at Chislehurst, illustrated in the last chapter (Figs. 313 and 314). The remaining pictures in this chapter illustrate good and simple pieces of furniture in various manners for differing types of garden design.

CHAPTER XXI.—ROCK GARDENS.

(Contributed by Mr. Raymond E. Negus.)

Modern Rock Gardening—Principles of Design—Stratification—Formation of the Rock Garden—Kinds of Rock—Likes and Dislikes of Alpines—Planting—Shrubs—Situation of the Rock Garden— Uses of Rockwork—Pools—Bog Gardens—Paths—Steps—Moraines.

THE charms of rock gardening are so many and so varied that no owner of a garden should fail to devote some small portion of the space at his disposal to the culture of alpines and rock plants if the site lends itself to such treatment. In spite of the mass of literature upon the topic the true principles upon which practice should be based are little appreciated to-day. The rock garden, unlike many other forms of horticulture, is a deliberate imitation of Nature; nine-tenths of our rock gardens, if they imitate Nature at all, imitate her in her least pleasing moods, for they represent formless heaps of rubble. Every stone in the garden should bear the semblance of having been in its place from time immemorial. The first principle of rock gardening is, " Adopt a definite scheme of stratification and carry it out uniformly throughout your garden." In Nature, it is true, a few kinds of rock, such as granite, are unstratified; but they are rarely suitable for rock garden-

FIG. 359.—OUTCROP OF STRATIFIED ROCK AT CORNERS.

ing. The stones used should be of the largest possible size compatible with convenience of handling. It is of the utmost importance that a stone once placed in position should never be moved; moreover, large, well-placed rocks are a joy in and for themselves (see Fig. 361), whereas small ones almost invariably look scrappy. Large rocks afford a firm foothold by which you may hop nimbly from ledge to ledge and use deft fingers to advantage without leaving a footmark, and without inflicting injury on tender growths.

Fig. 362 affords an example of the errors into which neglect of right principles leads the maker of a rock garden. In the foreground are several

FIG. 360.—ROCKS PROPERLY STRATIFIED AND SKILFULLY LAID.

FIG. 361.—BOLD STRATIFIED ROCKWORK AND MASS-PLANTING.

FIG. 362.—ROCKS ILL-PLACED WITHOUT UNIFORMITY OR ENOUGH SPACE FOR PLANTS.

FIG. 363.—TREATMENT OF AN ODD CORNER.

dozen clumps of choice silvery and mossy saxifrages, but the rocks, though large and good, are so placed that not only do they fail to please, but they do not readily permit of proper planting. Stones properly stratified, on the other hand, are admirably adapted to the needs of the plants. The best all-round kind of rock to employ is weather-worn limestone, which is beautiful in itself. Natural stone should be used wherever it occurs in the district. Sandstone crumbles somewhat rapidly, but the grit thus produced is a valuable rooting medium. Avoid, as you would the plague, all manner of brickbats, clinkers, concrete and tree trunks. Always lay the stones with their broadest face downwards. If these

simple rules be obeyed, the rock garden will appear to be something inherent in the soil, and not a mere fortuitous medley of stones. It is desirable that all the rocks should dip the same way. It used to be thought that it was necessary to have all stones dipping backward into the soil, but experience has shown that this is not so. The reverse slope shown in Fig. 367 at A will conserve moisture quite as effectually as the slopes indicated at C and E. The formation shown also in Fig. 367 by B and D has been found successful from every point of view. The actual appearance of rocks laid as shown by C and E is seen in Figs. 359 and 360 respectively. The whole of the soil underlying the rock garden must be thoroughly trenched and worked to a depth of at least two and a half feet, and deeper still if possible. Plenty of leaf mould, or thoroughly rotten manure, should be incorporated in the soil.

FIG. 364.—ALPINE PRIMULAS GROWING IN VERTICAL FISSURE.

FIG. 365.—ALPINE PRIMULAS GROWING IN HORIZONTAL FISSURE.

Alpines, almost without exception, revel in a deep, rich, cool soil. No trouble should be spared to ensure thorough preparation. The great enemies of the dainty mountain plants are damp and drought. A deep, well-worked, porous soil will do more towards preventing fatalities than any amount of artificial drainage and superficial watering. Practically the whole of the alpine flora has an intense dislike of a stiff or retentive soil. All soil used for planting should contain a goodly admixture of sharp sand or grit. For the lime - lovers, such as the encrusted saxifrages, lime, if possible in the form of old mortar rubble, should be incorporated in the compost. All alpines dislike wet about the collar. A top-dressing one inch in thickness of small granite chips will do much to save them from this danger, and will

FIG. 366.—A ROUGH RETAINING WALL.

also prevent undue evaporation in hot weather. The greatest care must be taken in planting. Some alpines are extremely fastidious during the early days of their career, and trouble taken at this stage is well bestowed. Many disappointments are due to the unsatisfactory condition in which plants are received. It is worth while to pay a slightly higher price and make sure of getting plants in good condition and well packed. Other failures are due to planting too late in the autumn. Experience shows that the best of all times for planting is the late spring, unless it can be done early in a wet September, due regard being had to peculiar conditions. What is best in one county may be disastrous in another. Void spaces left behind rocks are fatal to the well-being of any plants whose roots penetrate into them. For this reason light, friable, porous soil should be used, since it can be

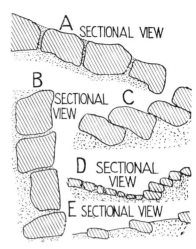

FIG. 367.—ROCK FORMATIONS.

well rammed between and behind the stones without fear of its caking. If the stock of plants is ready to hand, so that planting and building can be done at the same time, so much the better. The smaller and younger the plants the more likely they are to take kindly to their new surroundings. Old, well-established clumps are a snare, while the rapidity with which even notoriously difficult subjects increase if once they

FIG. 368.—THE KEYNOTE OF SUCCESS IN PLANTING IS SIMPLICITY.

FIG. 369.—" PLANT IN BOLD MASSES."

FIG. 370.—LARGE CLUMPS GIVE AN APPEARANCE OF SOLIDITY.

FIG. 371.—BOLD MASSES OF ROCK AND PLANTS.

be persuaded to settle down when quite young is amazing. Not a chink in the rockwork but should be filled with vegetation. Alpine primulas make splendid crevice plants for the cool side of the garden.

In all rock gardens, whether great or small, the keynote of success in planting, as in building, is simplicity. The majority of rock gardens are mere botanical collections, interesting but not beautiful. If means are limited, fewer kinds of plants may be acquired, but many examples of those kinds, or, better still, seedlings may be raised and then planted in bold masses. In a small rock garden ambitious schemes, unless they be faultless in every detail, are doomed to failure. An intelligent reproduction of some corner which has struck

FIG. 372.—A JUDICIOUS USE OF COMPACT SHRUBS.

FIG. 373.—RETAINING OR BOUNDARY WALL OF ROUGH UNHEWN BLOCKS.

FIG. 374.—BOUNDARY WALL WITH ITS TOP PLANTED WITH SHRUBS.

the eye with pleasure may well result in the creation of a delightful effect. A judicious use of compact shrubs will add greatly to that appearance of solidity which every rock garden should present. In a well-planned rockery the eye should not see too much at a time, but should be gently led from one prospect to another. Suitable shrubs further this purpose. The larger heaths are useful, and Japanese maples are indispensable, providing rich colour in autumn. The cistuses and their lesser brethren, the helianthemums, are good but rampant, the cistuses requiring plenty of headroom. The prostrate cotoneasters and dwarf kinds of cytisus are among the best, as are Gaultheria procumbens and Pernettya mucronata. One of the most charming of all small shrubs is Daphne Cneorum, with its innumerable fragrant pink blossoms. The lesser genistas and veronicas, especially V. Hectori, are useful. Skimmia japonica is decorative in winter with its red berries, and at all seasons valuable for its excellent foliage. The shrubby spiræas, such as arguta multiflora and prunifolia, are splendid in every way. The list of suitable shrubs is a long one, but there should in every case be a goodly number of dwarf conifers of the Savin class, such as Juniperus compressus nanus and the ordinary J. Sabina. Very choice, delicate plants should be grown in a portion of the garden specially allotted to them, in order to avoid risk of their becoming overwhelmed and lost. Very many of the choicest species succeed best in the moraine. It is a common but misguided practice to plant yuccas in the rock gardens. No plants are more hopelessly out of keeping with the general character. These and any plant or shrub which has anything of a tropical aspect must be rigidly excluded.

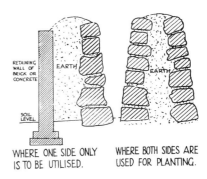

FIG. 375.—BOUNDARY WALLS.

No difficulty should be experienced in respect of the situation of the rock garden, for there are numberless species to suit every aspect. The shade, and even the proximity, of trees must be carefully avoided. Generally speaking, the more open and exposed the situation the better, provided some sort of shelter can be furnished against cutting or excessively boisterous winds. In every case the rock garden should be as far as possible from the dwelling-house, and the transition to it should be gradual. It is a great mistake to cramp the rock garden unless the space available is very circumscribed, for the greater the freedom the greater will be the illusion of reality. Furthermore, nearly all alpines love light and air.

There are various forms of rock garden, such as the dell, the ravine, the miniature cliff, the knoll. Many different types will be found in the illustrations. Even in the smallest backyard there is scope for a square yard or two of such construction as is seen in Figs. 359, 360 and 363. The mere fact of its being an odd corner should not

FIG. 376.—BOG AND WATER GARDEN.

FIG. 377.—A GOOD ROCK POOL.

be an excuse for hasty workmanship. There is a use to which rockwork is seldom put, namely, as a boundary wall. It is true considerable trouble and expense are entailed, because such a wall must ordinarily be double, with at least two feet of good soil between the faces. The second face should be of rock or brick or concrete, according as it is or is not visible from the garden. The method of construction is illustrated in Fig. 375, and examples are to be seen in Figs. 366, 373 and 374. A perforated pipe led along the top of the wall will make it a suitable home for the choicest subjects. Failing that expedient, the soil should consist largely of peat, sand and leaf-mould, with but a small proportion of loam. Water properly employed forms a charming feature in any rock garden. Few things are more delightful than the reflection in still water of overhanging rocks clothed with masses of blossom. A good example may be seen in Fig. 377.

FIG. 378.—STEPPING-STONES.

A little cascade, such as appears in Fig. 379, can sometimes be arranged. Where space permits, a path may be led down to the edge of a pool, and carried across by means of stepping-stones, as in Fig. 378.

No rock garden is complete without a space of boggy ground, for many gems, such as primulas farinosa and rosea, are never completely happy under other conditions than those afforded by moist ground. The type of pond illustrated in Fig. 380 has been found admirably adapted to the needs of the small garden. Upon the margins contained within the actual boundaries of the pond Japanese

FIG. 379.—BOLD STRATIFIED ROCKWORK AND SMALL CASCADE.

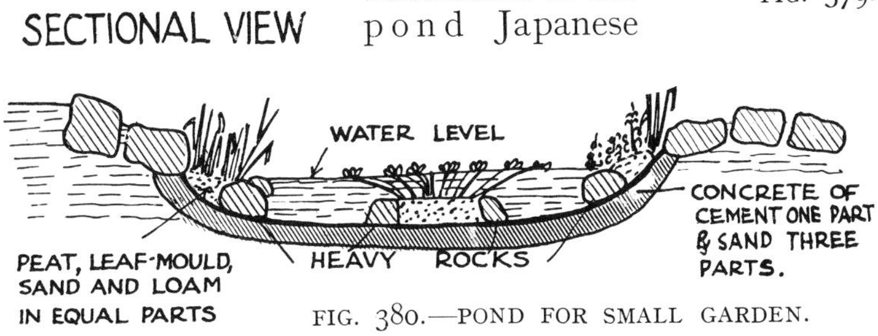

SECTIONAL VIEW

WATER LEVEL

CONCRETE OF CEMENT ONE PART & SAND THREE PARTS.

PEAT, LEAF-MOULD, SAND AND LOAM IN EQUAL PARTS

HEAVY ROCKS

FIG. 380.—POND FOR SMALL GARDEN.

irises, primulas, dodecatheons and other moisture-loving plants will flourish. Primula rosea grown in this way is a prodigy of vigour and abundant bloom. A typical bog

FIG. 381.—A ROCKY PATH.

and water garden is seen in Fig. 376, but such a conception can only be carried out where there is a good stream. With a little forethought in planning and construction, however, a wonderful illusion of spaciousness may be produced in a small area.

As to paths in the rock garden, the best form is that seen in Fig. 381, but it is somewhat expensive to make. It is, however, one with the garden, and is beautiful in itself, not a hideous and anomalous intrusion, as is the common gravel path. A paved path, as in Fig. 382, is another good type. Fig. 369 shows what may be called "land stepping-stones." The slabs of stone which form the path, instead of being let in flush with the surface of the soil, are left projecting some eight

FIG. 382.—A ROUGH PAVED PATH.

or nine inches. The interspaces are filled with dwarf flowers, and thus one may walk over a veritable sea of blossom without so much as damaging a petal. Failing the rocky or stone path, the best kind is of grass. In many respects it is more natural than any other kind, and serves as a setting to the rocks and their vegetation. The amount of labour entailed is somewhat heavy, and care should be taken that no rock is placed within six inches of the verge of the grass, otherwise the edges will need to be trimmed by hand.

Where the garden lies on a slope it may be terraced, the terraces being supported by retaining walls of rock, preferably constructed of large unhewn blocks after the manner described in Chapter XII. The secret of success is to have a thick layer

FIG. 383.—CYPRIPEDIUMS THOROUGHLY AT HOME ON THE UPPER MARGIN OF A ROCK GARDEN.

FIG. 384.—ROCK STEPS LEADING FROM TERRACE THROUGH ROCK
WALL TO ROCK GARDEN.

of rich compost behind the rock face. Fig. 384 shows the charming effect of roughly-hewn rocky steps leading down through such a wall from the terrace to the rock garden. Such steps should not be allowed to become overgrown with herbage, though small fry, like Erinus alpinus, Ionopsidium acaule and Linaria alpina, may be suffered to grow in the interstices. In the small bog garden one must carefully avoid such vigorous growers as Gunnera, Rodgersia, Saxifraga peltata and all those plants which appear in catalogues under the heading "Bog and Waterside Plants." The bog should be devoted to Primulas rosea, cockburniana, farinosa, frondosa, japonica, pulverulenta, capitata, denticulata, Sieboldii; to shortias, terrestrial orchids, the choicer trolliuses, dodecatheons and mertensias.

The soil must be spongy and constantly moist, but at the same time well drained, for nothing worth growing will endure stagnant moisture. A few large, flat slabs of stone on the surface will be of great value in affording access to all parts of the bog without injury to the plants. Fig. 383 shows cypripediums thoroughly at home upon the upper margin of a bog garden. A moraine garden is troublesome to construct, but repays the trouble. The essentials are very sharp drainage and abundance of moisture in dry weather. Unless the supply of water is very limited,

FIG. 385.—CONSTRUCTION OF SMALL MORAINE.

it is not necessary to have the concrete foundation shown in Fig. 385, although the latter is the best form for the small moraine, affording the most complete control over the water supply. In wet weather the inlet pipe is shut and the outlet opened; in dry weather the converse. Where a slope is available, Fig. 386 shows a simple but efficient type of moraine. A half-inch pipe perforated at every six inches is led along the top six inches below the surface. Flat rocks are useful, as in the bog garden, for access to the plants. Fig. 387 shows the construction of a moraine which has been found to work well in practice.

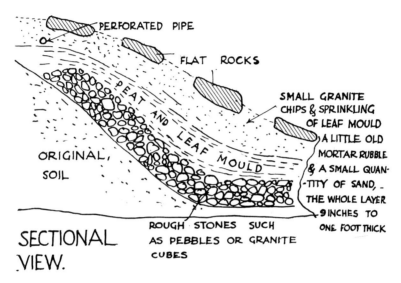

FIG. 386.—CONSTRUCTION OF MORAINE ON SLOPE.

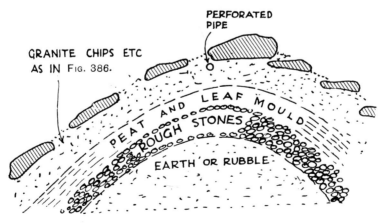

FIG. 387.—CONSTRUCTION OF MORAINE ON LEVEL GROUND.

INDEX.

Note.—The LARGE *numerals indicate* ILLUSTRATIONS *of the subject indexed, and refer not to the Figure numbers, but to the* PAGES *on which illustrations will be found. The* SMALL *numerals indicate* REFERENCES IN THE TEXT.

Index. 259

Note.—The LARGE *numerals indicate* ILLUSTRATIONS *of the subject indexed, and refer not to the Figure numbers, but to the* PAGES *on which illustrations will be found. The* SMALL *numerals indicate* REFERENCES IN THE TEXT.